"ᐧ
on a
the an
that cha
about it. We will definitely ı
more teens ab·ut God's love ɑ
the only One wh·ɔ can make a
have enjoyed getting to know ⅼ
genuine and has a deep desire

D1580557

-- *Debbi Witt, Co-Founder/Associate Director of Teen Quest (www.teenquest.org)*

Wow. This is an awesome resource for girls. Praise God! I have a blog that I posted one of your videos on, as well as a link to your website. I pray that it encourages the girls that see it and that they check out this website. It's really an amazing resource (I wouldn't put it up there for them if I didn't think it would be spiritually edifying for them).

-- *S'ambrosia, author of datelesswonders.blogspot.com*

I think what you've done is amazing! This is a really informational site, really uplifting and it's terrible yet comforting to know so many other girls feel the same way I do! It's great you have so many opportunities for your viewers to contribute as well! Shelley, you must be a really caring person and I appreciate this site so much!! Thank you! God is most definitely using you well.

--*Meghan*

Mirror Mirror...
Am I Beautiful?

Looking Deeper to
Find Your True Beauty

Mirror Mirror…Am I Beautiful?

Copyright © 2008 by Shelley Hitz

Printed in the United States of America
ISBN   1440457727

Additional copies can be ordered at:
www.truebeautybook.com.

Learn more information about Shelley's ministry at:
www.ShelleyHitz.com

Presented to:

From:

Date:

I dedicate this book to the One who has rescued me from destruction...Jesus Christ. He is my first love and my Savior. Without Him, I am nothing.

I also thank my husband, CJ, who continues to love, encourage and support me on this journey.
I thank God for you every day!!

Isaiah 61:1, 4
"The Spirit of the Sovereign LORD is on me,
because the LORD has anointed me
to preach good news to the poor.
He has sent me to bind up the brokenhearted,
to proclaim freedom for the captives
and release from darkness for the prisoners...

They will rebuild the ancient ruins
and restore the places long devastated;
they will renew the ruined cities
that have been devastated for generations."

CONTENTS

Part One

Find Your True Beauty

Introduction
Did you know...

- 24% of women would sacrifice 3 years of their life to be thin.
- Girls as young as five have expressed fears of getting fat.
- 90% of high school junior and senior girls diet regularly even though only between 10-15% are considered overweight.

Does this surprise you? Do you wonder why this is happening?

I believe one of the biggest influences on girls today regarding beauty is the media.

The reason I decided to write this book is to help you recognize these influences and discover your true beauty. It's always been there, it just needs to be found and rescued.

What is the one question all girls ask, even from a small age?

"Am I Beautiful?"

I remember that my dream as a young girl was to be "Miss America." At our slumber parties in my basement, we would actually hold our own Miss America contests...dressing up and coming down the steps to the familiar tune of "Here she comes, Miss America."

Unfortunately, we become disillusioned by life and the lies from the media destroy our hope....the hope that we will be found beautiful.

Girls, it's time to relight our hope and find our true beauty!

We need to uncover the lies we've believed and replace them with the truth. "Then you will know the truth and the truth will set you free." John 8:32

Jesus invites us to take this journey to discover our true beauty. Let's embark on this journey together. Will you join me? I'll be your guide, but we will both have many stories to share along the way. I look forward to sharing mine and hearing yours.

Advertising and body image....is there a connection? As a teen girl, do you think it is fair that the media portrays an unrealistic "perfect image" for how you should look? How do you think this impacts your self esteem and body image?

Share your opinion and read what others have to say here:

http://Share.TrueBeautyBook.com

The Truth About Beauty

What is the truth about beauty?

Well, let's start by looking at the word authentic. It's another word for truth or true. Authenticity, what is it?

Think of it this way...would you rather have a homemade turkey Thanksgiving dinner or a frozen TV dinner? Would you rather have a genuine diamond ring or one with cubic zirconium? It's a no brainer, right? We want the real stuff. The authentic. But, so often, in life, I give in and settle for less than the best. I choose the TV dinner and the cubic zirconium.

What is authenticity? What does it mean to be genuine? I believe it's being able to accept myself and be who I was created to be. It's not about what others think of me or even what others want me to be. *It's about being who I was created to be.* That's where I begin to find the truth about beauty.

So, what was I created to be? What were you created to be?

Hmmm...this is a question that has stumped me many times. Let's just brainstorm a little bit.

I know I was created by Jesus and for Jesus. "For by him all things were created: things in heaven and on earth, visible and invisible, whether thrones or powers or rulers or authorities; *all things were created by him and for him.*" Colossians 1:16

13

So I was created to be God's creation. I was created to be in a relationship with Jesus. What else?

Romans 8:16-17 says, "The Spirit himself testifies with our spirit that *we are God's children*. Now if we are children, then we are heirs—heirs of God and co-heirs with Christ."

Therefore, I am created to be God's daughter and as the daughter of a King, a Princess. With this role come both privileges and responsibilities. But, is there more?

Ephesians 3:19 says, "And to know this love that surpasses knowledge—*that you may be filled to the measure of all the fullness of God*." The Amplified version says, "flooded with God Himself." I am created to be filled to the measure with God's love. That means there are no empty spots. My life is created to be full, not empty.

I am created for the display of God's splendor (Isaiah 61:3). I am created to be a reflection of Him. I am created to become more and more like my Father. The real deal.

I am created to be beautiful.

Whoa...did that catch anyone else off guard? It did me. So many times I don't feel beautiful. I feel the opposite. Homely and average. But, not always beautiful. Created to be beautiful? That one is sometimes hard to believe. But, it's true.

What is authentic beauty...true beauty?

And why am I afraid to embrace my true beauty? Why do I instead do the easy thing and settle for so much less, striving for outward beauty and the world's approval of how I look? Because it's the easy thing.

Just like popping a TV dinner in the microwave is easier than cooking a full blown turkey dinner for Thanksgiving. It will not have the same rewards and results, but it's easier.

Plus, our culture screams at us from every billboard, commercial, TV program, movie, magazine, etc. that our outer beauty is more important than our true beauty. That to be valued by others, we have to "look" a certain way. They are teaching us to settle for what they say beauty is instead of embracing the truth about beauty, our authentic and true beauty given to us by our Creator.

This is a picture I get of my true beauty.

I see my beauty radiating from the inside out. That when I love God with all my heart, soul, strength and mind (Matthew 22:37), it will naturally spill over to all my relationships and every area of my life. It's as if God's light and beauty is in my heart. And it is being pumped into every cell of my body, my brain, my muscles, my organs through my bloodstream. And as long as God's Spirit is living inside of me, I will have that beauty radiating from the inside out. People will see the light in my eyes. They'll be drawn to the joy in my smile. And they'll want to find comfort in my friendship.

What about you?

Have you been settling for this world's beauty instead of discovering your true beauty? If so, I encourage you to discover the truth about beauty! Ask God to help you change your thoughts and desires about beauty. And He will. It may not be instant, but He will slowly begin to change you from the inside out!

Self Esteem

Why Do We Struggle So Much?

There's emptiness in many girls around this globe, what is the problem? We struggle with insecurity. We are ashamed of how we look.

In fact, I have a quiz on my website where over 50% of girls admit that they are ashamed of how they look. Over fifty percent!

There is a problem.

Don't believe me? Check out these body image statistics I found in Dr. Deborah Newman's book, "Comfortable in your own skin, making peace with your body image[1]." These statistics show the depth of our problem.

1. Americans had 11 million cosmetic plastic surgery procedures in 2006 - up 7%.[2]

2. More than half of teenage girls are, or think they should be, on diets. They want to lose some or all of the 40 pounds that females naturally gain between ages 8 and 14. About 3% of these teens go too far, becoming anorexic or bulimic.[3]

3. The *Medical Journal of Psychiatry* conducted a general population study on men with eating disorders and found that 2% of men, compared to 4.8% of women, have anorexia or bulimia.[4]

4. The average American woman is 5'4" tall and weighs 140 pounds, while the average American model is 5'11" tall and weighs 117 pounds. Most fashion models are thinner than 98% of American women.[5]

5. 80% of American women are dissatisfied with their appearance.[6]

6. Female athletes are six times more likely to develop eating disorders than other women.[7]

7. 80% of women say that the images of women on television and in movies, fashion magazines, and advertising makes them feel insecure.[8]

8. 42% of girls first through third grades want to be thinner.[9]

9. 81% of 10 year olds are afraid of being fat.[10]

10. Without treatment, up to 20% of people with serious eating disorders die. With treatment, that number falls to 2 to 3%.[11]

• The average woman spends 2 1/2 years of her life washing, styling, cutting, coloring, crimping, and straightening her hair at home and in the salon.[12]

Wow Am I Fat or What!
By Amber

I have not always thought I was fat. My addiction with my size did not start until my freshman year in high school. It seems as though once I started verbally abusing myself I could not stop.

At first I would say, "Oh, if I only lose 10 pounds I would look so much better and I would have so many more friends. And maybe (insert a guy's name) would even talk to me more." Then I looked in the mirror again and said, "Wow my head is way too small for my body size. I just need to even it out, and then I'll look better."

This constant self bashing continued, and got worse than ever when I heard that some of my so called friends had been talking about me. This cycle continued until the middle of the semester when I got a boyfriend. Our relationship made me feel better. It made me feel like I was pretty because he liked me and I thought that someone saying I was pretty or beautiful made it true.

This feeling of self worth was soon dashed when I found out that he wanted to break up with me. I came up with so many reasons why he would break up with me: my hair, my stomach, basically everything but my honey brown eyes were the problem.

I went through the rest of the term fine. I eventually got over it and moved on, but I still held on to my self hate with my body weight. All my real friends would tell me that I was not fat; I was "thick." And my best friend told me that the only real body problem I had was that I thought I was fat when I wasn't.

She said that "No, you aren't skinny but you are most definitely not fat."

This year I am a sophomore and I go to a new school that I hate with a passion. Where I always end up comparing myself to someone else and not being myself. I feel like I can't wear this or that because I'm not a size 6 or 7.

And I know that the reason that I may not have as many friends is not because I'm over weight, but because I don't love myself enough to let people into my shell. I am very surprised at myself that I am even writing this, so hope you read it.

I feel that I need to start loving myself no matter what I weigh because I know that God made me special and I look the way I do for a reason. And even if I am overweight I should not stress about it and deal with it by working out and eating better. And reading God's word so that when someone says something mean about me it won't matter because I will know that I am beautiful and that God loves me.

P.S I don't think I'm ugly I just think I could lose some weight. :)

Amber,
I am so glad you were able to share this with us! Part of the battle is secrecy...for instance mold grows best in darkness. So, just writing this helps to break some of the strength of this struggle in your life.

I want to share this verse as encouragement...
Isaiah 61:1 "The Spirit of the Sovereign LORD is on me, because the LORD has anointed me to preach good news to the poor. He has sent me to bind up the brokenhearted, to proclaim freedom for the captives and release from darkness for the prisoners."

~Shelley

Feeling Empty Inside

I have felt this emptiness before. For me, it tends to be a *deep loneliness* that threatens to engulf me. I often feel left out and rejected. I feel like I am on the outside. Even though I have loving and meaningful relationships, it isn't enough. I still have that gaping hole inside. For you it may feel different, but I bet it's still there. Some of you may not even know it's there. I lived with it for many years before I recognized it.

So, What's the Problem?

Ultimately, the problem is that we are trying to find our self esteem and worth *apart from God.* "All things were created by him and for him" (Colossians 1:16). That hole inside us is meant to be filled by God and so nothing else will be enough. We will always still feel "hungry" for more.

I tried to get my worth from many other things....my relationships (husband, family, and friends), my work (succeeding at what I do), my looks (clothes, make-up, hair, etc.), attention from guys, shopping, etc. We can try to fill this emptiness and void with anything and everything. Many of those things can become addictions over time. I've had a couple of those too.

And that is the enemy's purpose. He has come to steal kill and destroy us (John 10:10). He wants to plant many weeds in our lives to choke out the life giving, fruit bearing plants.

However, I do believe there are other influences in our culture today that also contribute to this emptiness inside us. And I believe one of the biggest issues impacting us today is the pressure the media places on us to look "picture perfect."

Barbie Body Image

How toys like Barbie influence our body image

How many girls have grown up playing with Barbie dolls? A lot. Statistics show that two Barbie's are sold every second somewhere in the world. In fact, the average American girl from ages 3 to 11 owns 10. [13]

Barbie's Body Type

If you met Barbie as a human being, what would she look like? Well, there are differing views.

One source says Barbie would stand about 5'6", weigh nearly 120 pounds, and have the measurements 38-18-34 (38 inches for her chest - 18 inches at her waist - 34 at her hips).

It is speculated that if Barbie were human, she would be so thin that she would not be able to menstruate or have her monthly cycle. This is because she would not have the body fat needed to do so.[14] Statistics say the Barbie's body type is likely to occur in one out of every 100,000 women.[15]

No matter how you look at it, Barbie's body is not average, and is not easily attainable.

Barbie's Impact

What impact does this have on young girls that spend hours and hours playing with these dolls? Do they want to become like Barbie and look like her?

We know that the more time we spend with anything, the more influence it has on us. If you spend weeks studying for a test, you'll probably do better than if you just spend a few minutes studying.

I think the same is true with our time. If we spend hours and hours playing with Barbie dolls, they are bound to have an influence on us. Just as if we would spend hours and hours playing video games.

Barbie Body Image...One Woman's Quest to Become Barbie

There is one woman, Cindy Jackson, who was so influenced by Barbie that it became her life mission to look exactly like her. Her obsession to look like Barbie started when her parents bought her first Barbie at the age of 6.

And she didn't give up until she reached her goal. She ended up spending about $55,000 and underwent 20 plastic surgery operations to reach her goal of becoming Barbie.[16]

20 operations!

This is just one more example of how impossible it is to reach this ideal image without major alterations of our natural beauty.

A 1965 Barbie Body Image Message

I couldn't believe this when I read it....In 1965 Mattel came out with a "Slumber Party Barbie" that came complete with a bathroom scale permanently set at 110 pounds.

The doll also came with a book entitled "How to Lose Weight" and inside this book it gave the advice: "Don't Eat". The matching Ken doll also came with slumber party accessories, but his were milk and cookies, sending a very different message.[17]

Barbie Transformed

Mattel received many criticisms about Barbie and the impact she was having on young girls around the world. In the summer of 2000, they decided to change Barbie to a more modern look.

"The new Barbie will have a more natural body shape – less busty with wider hips."

What caused Mattel to make these changes? One influence may have been a drop in sales. According to the Los Angeles Business Journal, Barbie sales dropped from $2 billion to $1.5 billion in 1999.[18]

What about you?

What influences in your life have shaped the way you see your body image? Consider the media you take in on a daily basis: the magazines you read, the websites you surf and the television shows you watch. How does seeing all these images impact you and your self esteem? Are there any changes you need to make in your media choices?

Share Your Thoughts

Share Your Reactions to Barbie. Do you think Barbie influences girls today? Do you think playing with dolls like Barbie gives us an unrealistic "standard" of what we should look like?

Share your opinion and read what others have to say here:

http://Share.TrueBeautyBook.com

Body Image Lies

Have You Fallen for This One?

I think as females, most of us have struggled with body image lies, especially this one.

Body Image Lie:

If I can change something about my body, others will finally accept me and I will be able to accept myself.

It is so easy to base our self worth on our looks and our outer appearance because it is the first thing others see in us.

Plus, there are mirrors (or windows) everywhere that constantly remind us of our appearance.

As I started to work on this area in my life, I realized one day that I was addicted to mirrors. I was always checking my appearance to see if I looked okay. Some days I would feel good about what I saw and thought that my hair and/or outfit was cute. However, there were other days I couldn't wait to get home and hide.

Ever feel this way?

Note: One way to know whether or not you are also addicted to mirrors is to deliberately try to avoid them for a day or two. Like me, you may realize it's more of an obsession, or "addiction", than you realized.

25

What Would You Change About Your Body?

What if you could change one thing about your body, what would you change?

I know my answer without even thinking about it. I bet most of you already know your answer too.

The thing I've struggled with the most has been my acne and the scars it has left behind.

In high school I had a perfect complexion. I even remember someone commenting that my skin looked like a china doll. Well, that soon ended when I entered college.

I'm not sure exactly what caused it -- possibly the combination of bad eating habits and hormones. I thought it would just be a short phase and then be gone. But, here I am, now in my 30's and still struggling with breakouts of acne.

UUUGGGGHHHH!!

I've tried most everything from Mary Kay to ProActiv to Arbonne to supplements and vitamins to hormone creams, etc. Nothing has worked. Plus, I have the scars that the acne has left behind to look at every day in the mirror.

So, how did I cope? To compensate for the acne and try to cover it up, I began wearing a lot of makeup.

One day I felt challenged by God to go out to eat with my husband, CJ, without wearing any makeup. I wasn't sure I understood correctly. Go without any makeup?? Surely not.

So I asked God, "Are you sure you want me to do this?"

You see, I was using makeup as a means of self-protection and to feel better about myself. So to go out without any makeup literally felt like I was leaving the house naked! How embarrassing and devastating!

Well, anyway, I did end up obeying God that night and left without a trace of makeup. After a few minutes, I couldn't stand it any longer, so I asked my husband if he noticed anything different about my appearance.

He looked at me and hesitantly said, "You're wearing a new headband?"

I said, "Yes, I am wearing a new headband, but do you notice anything else about my appearance?" He said "No, I don't."

How ironic. Here I felt "naked" and self conscious and he didn't even notice!

What I learned from that experiment is that most people don't notice my imperfections nearly as much as I do. I'm much harder on myself.

What is The Truth?

The truth is that my value comes from God, my Creator, and not from my appearance and what others think of me.

God is teaching me this truth that my value comes from Him and not from my outward appearance. It is okay to desire beauty -- it's a God given desire – but not to base my self esteem on it.

Our Beauty Comes From God

I wanted to close with something a friend of mine, Annika Lampmann,[19] wrote.

"My precious daughter, your body is not an object.

I made you fearfully and wonderfully. My works are marvelous and your soul can believe this. (Psalms 139:14)

You are BEAUTIFUL and PERFECT, just as you are.

All beautiful you are, my darling; there is no flaw in you.
(Song of Solomon 4:7)

Look at yourself through my eyes and be amazed.

Your Dad, Your God, Your Creator.

Father, show me my beauty. Show me what you see when you look at me and show me what you put inside my heart. I want to be rooted in your love and bloom like a beautiful rose.

Fill me up with your spirit and with your thoughts. Let me see others and myself through your eyes, Jesus. Amen."

Here is Rehan's story...

```
I've always had a problem with my nose as it's too
big. Whenever I make new friends, I always get a
feeling that they don't like talking to me much
because of my physical appearance. I just don't
know how to deal with the loneliness and eternal
depression which I've had since I was 14 or so.

--Rehan
```

Overcoming the lies with the truth

Rehan,
Thanks for sharing so honestly. I know loneliness has been one of my deepest hurts. It connects back to some things that happened when I was a child.

Ultimately, I realized that I was "drinking from a broken cup - trying on my own to find satisfaction from life and that I really can only get that from God. God is healing me, but it is still a struggle not to believe the lie *that I am alone, that I don't fit with the others, that I am left out and on the outside, that I am different.*

In fact, just yesterday I was feeling that same thing again, believing that same lie again. And I wrote out the lie above and then I wrote out the truth.

The truth is *that I'm never alone. Jesus, my biggest fan and supporter, the life of the party, is always with me. I am always included in what Jesus is doing if I decide to join Him. I am Jesus' friend and he tells me his secrets and connects with me deeply.*

See the difference? Once I realized the lie I believed and replaced it with the truth, the melancholy feeling that came over me began to lift.

I want to share a few thoughts from the book "Comfortable in your own skin, making peace with your body image" by Dr. Deborah Newman. [20]

One thing she says is, "Your self-esteem isn't as much about how you look right now as it is about what you think about how you look right now."[21] She gave an example of how a woman lost a lot of weight and afterwards was asked out on a date.

The guy canceled and she automatically thought he canceled because he didn't like her and he thought she would gain all her weight back and wouldn't stay thin. Well, she came to find out that he really was sick and those thoughts were lies she still believed. Even though she had lost the weight, she still struggled with her self esteem.

The truth is "Healthy self esteem comes from believing in the value God places in you, not in the value man assigns to you."[22]

Another lie she addresses is that "My outward appearance is the most important thing about me... The truth: Your outward appearance is what people will first judge you by, but your personality, confidence, talents and abilities, and spiritual sensitivity are each vital to who you are as well."[23]

The last thing from her book I want to share is this. She says, "I like to think of our bodies as the garage for our souls, where we are parked temporarily while we live on this earth. The health, appearance, and abilities of our bodies affect what we do on this earth, but they are not all of who we are. They are significant to us for our time on earth, but will not last for eternity."[24]

Finally, check out these personalized verses and start reading them over and over. Allow them to soak into your mind!

You can download and print them at this link: www.personalpromisebible.com

Don't give up your search to finding your true beauty!

~Shelley

Luann shares her story...

I can definitely relate to Shelley's story about acne and stuff. I'm suffering from acne and acne scars too.

My self esteem is crashing down right now. Too bad I'm going to college. I have built this thing on my head saying that if only these blemishes were gone then everything would be alright.

It keeps haunting me night and day.

At first it didn't bother me but when my classmates started to tease me and then my maternal relatives started to humiliate me about it my world came crashing through. They tease me, even my 7 year old cousin.

I had depression too. I keep crying every night. Well not just that. My mom adds the pressure. She's always criticizing me and it did hurt me so bad. That's why I'm like this.

This person that I don't even know. This person who doesn't even know how to believe in herself and even though my dad keeps telling me I'm beautiful I never believe him because I know deep inside myself that I'm ugly as a monster.

I wanted to change this attitude towards myself because it's not helping me at all. It's destroying me. I get to only live once and I don't want to waste this chance.

It's really really hard to change and I definitely need your help. Can you help me recover? Let's help each other. Please I really need this so bad.

--*Luann*

A new kind of beauty...

Luann,
You are beautiful. I don't even need your picture
to see that. Every one of us is perfect in God's
eyes. I am so happy to be able to believe that
because I'm just starting to realize it myself. I
believe that with each and everyone one of us
women, we introduce the world to a new kind of
beauty. A new perfection. It comes with self
confidence and a trust in God. We must try to give
self consciousness to God. All of that gets in our
way with a relationship with Jesus.

You are in my prayers, along with every other girl
who feels the same way. (And you ARE gorgeous, my
dear.)

--*Kristin*

You are beautiful!

Luann,
It breaks my heart to hear what you're going
through. Especially for you to say "I know deep
inside myself that I'm ugly as a monster." That is
a lie. You are beautiful. The Bible says, that God
has made EVERYTHING beautiful in its time
(Ecclesiastes 3:11). That verse includes you,
Luann.

I prayed for you today, and I believe that God can
help you to overcome this difficult time in your
life when you seek Him.

Keep your head up!! You don't have to live under
the control of what others say about you!

--*Stacey*

Share Your Thoughts

How About You - What is One Thing You Want to Change About Your Body? Feel free to share how this has impacted your self esteem and your relationship with God or others.

The Lie: *"If I can change something about my body, others will finally accept me and I will be able to accept myself."*

You have read my story, as well as Amber's, Rehan's and Luann's stories...now it's time to tell yours. I look forward to hearing your stories!

Share your opinion and read what others have to say here:
http://Share.TrueBeautyBook.com

Other Articles Available Online:

Struggle with Anorexia? Read an article on anorexia here:
http://Anorexia.TrueBeautyBook.com

Struggle with Cutting? Read more on teenage cutting here:
http://Cutting.TrueBeautyBook.com

What Does the Bible Have to Say About Body Image?

1 Corinthians 6:19-20 "Do you not know that your body is a temple of the Holy Spirit, who is in you, whom you have received from God? You are not your own; you were bought at a price. Therefore honor God with your body.

Romans 12:2 "Do not conform any longer to the pattern of this world, but be transformed by the renewing of your mind. Then you will be able to test and approve what God's will is– his good, pleasing and perfect will."

1 Samuel 16:7 But the Lord said to Samuel, "Do not consider his appearance or his height, for I have rejected him. The Lord does not look at the things man looks at. Man looks at the outward appearance, but the Lord looks at the heart."

Psalms 139:14-16 "I praise you because I am fearfully and wonderfully made; your works are wonderful, I know that full well. My frame was not hidden from you when I was made in the secret place. When I was woven together in the depths of the earth, your eyes saw my unformed body. All the days ordained for me were written in your book before one of them came to be."

Philippians 3:20-21 "But our citizenship is in heaven. And we eagerly await a Savior from there, the Lord Jesus Christ, who, by the power that enables him to bring everything under his control, will transform our lowly bodies so that they will be like his glorious body."

Evolution vs. Creationism

Does it have an impact on our self esteem and body image?

We all know that there is a big debate about evolution vs. creationism in our culture today. I'm not here to debate.

What I am here to do is to challenge you to consider its impact on girls today. Is there a connection at all? Read on and you decide.

A Deeper Issue?

Is there more to the onslaught of low self esteem and body image issues teen girls and women face today? Could there be something deeper going on?

I think there is...

I believe there is a battle for our souls.

And I believe it is a spiritual battle. A battle against good and evil. A battle waging in the heavens against God and Satan. For you. For me.

It's subtle. Many times it comes through our thoughts. Subtle lies that we end up latching onto and believing.

Our enemy, Satan, may try to convince us to believe that...

- We have no real value and are worthless.
- We have no real beauty to offer to anyone and are ugly.
- We have no real purpose in life and our life is meaningless.
- We have no real relationships and no one truly cares about us.

Wow! Did you read those subtle lies?

Those thoughts can have major implications if we begin to bite into them...if we begin to believe them.

What is the result?

Broken, lifeless, defeated lives. We may experience sparks of real life from time to time, but in general we live with a deep ache inside. A sense that we don't belong. A sense that there's something wrong with us. Like I did for years.

The Connection to Evolution vs. Creationism

What if some of these thoughts could originate from something even deeper?

What if our enemy convinces us to believe that science has found the answer to how our universe began. And that if science can explain our origins, we don't need any other explanation. It's as if there's been a debate between science and God, and we've been told that science wins every time, hands down. And many of us have believed it.

What is the result?

We come to the conclusion that there is no need for an intelligent designer of our universe, that we are simply animals that evolved from lifeless cells millions of years ago.

You see, when we believe that there exists an intelligent designer or Creator of this universe that created us with love and value and thought, then we see ourselves differently.

How does evolution vs. creationism impact us in our search for true beauty and meaning in life? Think about it. If you evolved from lifeless, meaningless cells over millions of years, does your life really matter?

But what if there is more?

What if there is more to what we see all around us? Doesn't the beauty, complexity and magnificence of it all ever make you wonder?

I recently read something by Mark Cahill that made sense to me. He says, "every time we look at something built by man -- a house, for example -- we know it had a builder, someone who assembled it. When we see something that has design, like a watch, we know it had a designer who planned it. When we see artwork, like a painting, we know there is an artist who painted it. When we observe order -- say 20 Coke cups lined up in a row -- we know there was an "orderer" who set them up that way.

When we look around the universe at things not made by man, what do we see? We see creation, design, art, and order. So if everything man-made has a creator, designer, artist, or orderer behind it, why would you not think there is a Creator, Designer, Artist, and Orderer behind the universe?

Why is it that when we look at Mount Rushmore, we don't say 'Wow, erosion is an amazing thing! Look how it formed the heads of four presidents of the United States'? We realize that would be a foolish statement. Whenever we see creation, design, art, or order, it's obvious that there was some intelligent force behind it to make it happen."[25]

He then goes on to tell the story. "I was talking with a man one day in downtown Atlanta, and I asked him a question about spiritual matters. He replied that he was an atheist, and there was no way to prove there is a God. We were standing among tall buildings, so I pointed to one of the skyscrapers and said, 'Prove to me that there was a builder for that building.' He answered, 'That's easy. The building itself is proof that there is a builder.'

He was 100% correct. We know that you don't just gather some concrete, pipes, windows, paint, wires, etc., then turn around and look back to suddenly find a building. A building requires a builder.

I said, 'Exactly. The building is proof that there is a builder.' I then added, 'The sun, the moon, the stars, the oceans, the sand, each unique snowflake, the 3 billion pieces of your DNA that are different from mine, are absolute proof that there had to be a Creator of this universe.' He looked at me. I could see the light bulb flash on behind his eyes and then he glanced away. As he thought about the statement, he realized he had proved his own proof.

38

The fact that you can't see, touch, taste, smell, or hear the builder of a skyscraper doesn't mean that such a person doesn't exist. You don't need any amazing faith to believe there was a builder of a building you can see; you just need to look at the evidence and make an informed decision. And the best piece of evidence you have is the work that builder left behind.

The same holds true for the God of the universe. The evidence left for us to look at is all the evidence we will ever need in order to know that our universe has a Creator." [26]

So what if we had an intelligent designer, a Creator?

That would mean that...
• We are created with real value, and are worthwhile.
• We are created with true beauty to offer to others.
• We are created with real purpose and meaning in life.
• We are created to have meaningful relationships with our Creator and others.

See the difference?

If you're still struggling with the evolution vs. creationism idea, I recommend reading chapter two of Mark Cahill's book, *One Heartbeat Away, Your Journey into Eternity.*[27] He explains microevolution vs. macroevolution, transitional forms and more. It helped me better understand why Creation really does make sense when you truly take the time to examine the claims and evidence of evolution. I realized that it really does take more faith to believe in the evidence of evolution vs. creationism.

Now it's time for you to decide for yourself.

Daddy's Little Girl

The Importance of a Father's Love and What to Do if You Grew up Lacking It

You'll often hear someone say, "She's Daddy's little girl." Deep down, I think being "Daddy's little girl" is something we girls long for...to be loved, cherished and treasured by our fathers.

However, the reality is that many of us grew up without the stability, security and protection of a loving father. Instead, our fathers may have been distant emotionally, absent from the home, too busy working, abusive or neglectful. And we may have left childhood feeling unloved by our dads for one reason or another.

Fathers will have an impact on their daughter's life...

....either positively or negatively.

Don't get me wrong. A mother's nurturing love is essential. We need the love from both our mother and our father. But, our dads have a different impact on us.

- They teach us how to interact with guys.
- They teach us how a guy should treat a girl.

- They are the first man in our lives that has the opportunity to affirm our beauty and teach us that our beauty goes beyond skin deep.
- They model to us how a husband should treat his wife.
- And so on and so forth.

Did you feel secure in your father's love and protection growing up? Did you know that he had your best interests in mind? Did your dad affirm your beauty and worth and show you respect?

Unfortunately, many girls do not receive affirmation and love from their fathers. And therefore, it's easy to go looking for it somewhere else... usually trying to feel loved by other guys. You can read more about this when I share my story on dating.

The Impact on our Relationship with God

Sometimes we end up projecting our feelings about our earthly father onto our heavenly Father. If we feel like our earthy father is distant emotionally from us, we may assume that our heavenly Father is the same. If our earthly father has disappointed us and let us down, we may think that our heavenly Father will disappoint us as well. If our earthly father wasn't safe for us, but instead was abusive, we may have a difficult time trusting our heavenly Father to be a safe haven for us.

Do you see how this can happen?

I know it did for me. And I had to realize that God is not like my dad. He won't let me down or disappoint me. I had to be reminded of the character of God, my heavenly Father, through His Word, the Bible. It shows over and over that God is loving, trustworthy, and has my best interests in mind.

41

I had to slowly begin to change the way I saw God, or my view of God. You may have to do that as well.

You Can Have a Father that Loves You Completely

Are you longing for someone to love you completely and unconditionally? Well, before you try to find that love "in all the wrong places" like I did, realize that you can find that love in your heavenly Father. It may be hard for you to accept His love right now. You may not feel very love-able. Or you may doubt that God really cares for you.

It's okay to wrestle with those feelings. You are on a journey. A journey of discovering your true beauty. A beauty given to you by your heavenly Father, your Creator, who loves you completely. You were made by Him and for Him. (Col 1:16)

Will you allow Him to love you and satisfy all your deepest longings? Will you let go of your past and forgive your earthly father for the ways he didn't provide that love for you?

Your heavenly Father is waiting for you. He says, "Come near to me and I will come near to you." (James 4:8) He offers to love you completely (Ephesians 3:19) as a Father should. And nothing can separate you from His love (Romans 8:35-39)

Will you accept His invitation?

How To Gain Self Esteem...

By Breaking Free from the Lies We Believe

What do lies have to do with learning how to gain self esteem? Well, let me start by sharing an illustration. It has to do with weeds.

Let me ask you a question.

What is important when weeding a garden?

The recognition of which plants are weeds, right?

Otherwise, you may uproot the good with the bad or allow certain weeds to continue to take root, thinking they are life giving, fruit bearing plants!

Isn't the same is true in our lives, in regards to our thoughts? We need to develop "weed recognition", the ability to recognize when the enemy is planting those weeds of lies into our lives. Even Jesus said that they will know you by your fruit (Matthew 7:15-20).

In my life, this has made a huge difference as I've learned how to gain self esteem.

In his book, "Waking the Dead", John Eldredge[28] says, "most of us simply try to 'put things behind us,' get past it, forget the pain as quickly as we can. Really – denial is a favorite method for coping for many Christians. But not with Jesus. He wants truth in the inmost being, and to get it there he's got to take us into our inmost being....to go with him into the deep waters of the heart, uncover the lies buried down there, and bring in the truth that will set us free. Don't just bury it quickly; ask God what he is wanting to speak to."

Recognizing and uprooting the weeds or lies in your life is the first step in learning how to gain self esteem. Often times those thoughts that keep coming up in your mind again and again that tear you down instead of build you up will be those lies. In other words...."Stinkin' Thinkin'" as my mom calls it.

Realize that those defeating thoughts are not from God, but from your enemy, Satan, who wants to destroy you and keep you captive. (John 8:43-45, John 10:10, Isaiah 61:1-4)

Some examples of "Stinkin' Thinkin'":

- I am worthless
- People I trust will hurt and betray me, therefore I can't trust anyone
- I'm not as good as my friends
- Something's wrong with me
- I am ugly
- I have to be perfect for people to like me.
- I am a failure and always mess up.

In place of those lies, begin to plant the seed of God's truth into your mind (2 Corinthians 10:5). We are transformed by the renewing of our minds (Romans 12:2) and the only way to renew our minds is to change what goes into it.

Did you know that one way people are trained to recognize counterfeit money is by studying the real thing?

Therefore, one way we can get better at recognizing the lies is to know God's Truth in the bible so well that we can quickly recognize those thoughts that aren't from Him. Unfortunately, there is no shortcut for this step. The seed of truth may take time to grow, it's hard work but worth it!

One great way to do this is to memorize bible scriptures. I know it sounds boring, but think of it as a way to prepare for battle. I have found it to be one of the most effective ways for me to have victory over Satan in my life (see the appendix for more details).

Something else that has really helped me is praying God's word. If you are having difficulty overcoming a specific struggle in your life, I'd recommend trying it. It's changed my life (see the appendix for more details).

Starve the flesh and feed the spirit.

The more we feed the flesh, the bigger this "monster" grows and the more damage is seen. It seems innocent at first.

If you feel overwhelmed, don't! That's just another lie Satan is telling you to keep you from learning how to gain self esteem and true freedom in Christ. I have felt the same way and have had great friends to help me. You're not alone and if you need help or someone to listen, feel free to contact me.

Practical Steps to Replacing the Lies with Truth...[29]

1. **Identify possible lies** in your life. Pray for God's wisdom and ask someone you trust to help you. Write them out on a paper or journal.
2. **Choose** one of the lies.

3. **Confess** the sin of believing this lie rather than the truth and living your life according to this lie.
4. When applicable, **forgive** your parents or family members that have passed down this lie to you. Also, forgive any others that have influenced you to form this lie.
5. **Repent**, asking for God's forgiveness for living your life based upon this lie.
6. **Reject the lie** and break its power from your life based on what Jesus did for you by dying on the cross.
7. **Plant God's truth** into your mind in place of the lie. Write out this truth.
8. **Receive this new truth** into your belief system as the replacement for the previously removed lie. (repeat above steps until you have gone through the entire list of lies)
9. **Pray:**
   o Pray that God would bring an end to the effects of this lie in your life.
   o Pray for this truth to be planted in your heart.
   o Pray that the Word of God already in your heart will be brought to the surface of your mind to use as a weapon against future defeating thoughts. (Ephesians 6)
   o Pray for the discipline to meditate on this new truth for at least 30 days.
   o Pray that the Holy Spirit would make you sensitive to falling back into old thought patterns and to be able to take captive any such thoughts.
   o Pray for new habits to be formed in your mind as you learn how to gain self esteem.
10. **Accountability** – Have someone you trust hold you accountable.

Remember, this is just one step in learning how to gain self esteem. But, I can tell you from personal experience that it is powerful when you apply it.

Princess Kandace
by Kandace

It all started when I was in elementary school.
People made fun of my forehead and at first I
didn't think it was big but then I started
believing it since I heard it more. Middle school
was torture. I always had a boy who liked me that
would be mean to me. This particular boy who liked
me would pick fun at me. I didn't know why he
would be so mean and hurt my feelings but he did.

I cut my hair to make a bang so I could hide my
forehead. That solved my problems for a little
while. He still would make fun of me, only him. He
had a friend who he hung around with and his
friend thought I was cute and we were cool.

I would always compare myself to the popular
girls. I caught myself trying to be like other
girls. Why did all the cute guys like those girls?
Since I'm African American, guys are attracted to
girls who have big butts and loud mouths. I had
none of these traits.

That 7th grade summer I went to a camp for teens
with my church. That's when the healing began. I
started being my own self and I started getting
more friends. But I still had the forehead issue.
8th grade was still torture. This time it was a
new guy (the other one moved to Alabama). He was
kind of popular and that was kind of hurtful. He
was the class clown and he would clown on me,
knowing deep down he liked me. I wish I would've
known he liked me. I did however manage to get the
word of God known to some people at the school.

High school was the breaking point for me. I
started to get acne because I wore "swoops" and
bangs so much. One day in the 9th grade I was just
tired. I think God troubled my spirit so much that
I just put my bang back for the first time in my

life and did not care. That was the best thing I
could have ever done.

Yeah I got comments but I trusted God and you know
what, I didn't care what people had to say. Yeah
there was this guy who had a joke but I could've
cared less.

I've been showing my forehead for a year now and I
see nothing wrong with the way God made me. I look
at myself as unique, if I didn't have my forehead
or my eyes then I would look like guys expect me
to look like and I don't want that. I want to
look like KANDACE, a child of God, not some video
girl who has no significant value. Since my father
is a King I'm royalty, I'm a princess.

What is your story? How has God been working in your life
lately? It could be something big or something little. Share
your opinion and read what others have to say here:

http://Share.TrueBeautyBook.com

"Who Am I?"
Self Esteem Poem

by Shelley Hitz

I had an identity crisis several years ago and wrote this poem as I began to find my true identity. Maybe you can relate as well.

Who am I?

My first answer would probably be my name.

But, my name does not describe who I am on the inside. I could then give the title of my profession.

But that is what I do. I could then tell you I am a wife, a sister, and a daughter. But those are my relationships.

I ask again...Who am I?

I could describe myself as an extrovert and outgoing. That is my personality. I am organized in planning events. But that is a gift God has given me. I could describe my appearance, but that is not who I am either.

So many times I have believed what others say I am. If I receive affirmation, then I feel worthwhile.

However, when I receive criticism, then I feel like a failure. I have chosen to ride the roller coaster of emotions, Instead of believing the truth of what God says about me. I have tried to work harder to prove that I am worthwhile. Yet every time I mess up or fail, I am reminded that I will never measure up.

I will never be pretty enough or talented enough. I will never be skinny enough or do enough good things of the church. I will never be a good enough wife or sister or daughter.

But, I keep trying harder and harder. I believe the lie that if I continue to try harder, I will finally be "good" enough.

One day, God gently said to me, "Stop trying so hard to prove yourself to others. Get your worth from me. I've already given it to you. Remember my grace. It's a free gift and nothing you can achieve by trying harder.

Rest in my grace.

You are working so hard to have a certain position in the eyes of others, To be well-liked and to have popularity. You want to be appreciated for what you do.

But I want you to know that you already have an elevated position.

Because you have a relationship with my son, Jesus Christ, You are a part of my kingdom as my daughter, and co-heirs with Christ. Because you are the daughter of a King, You are given the position of being a princess.

You are my princess, a royal princess.

Remember that an earthly princess is not special because of who she is or what she does. She has status and position because of who her dad is, a king. She has royalty in her blood.

You have royalty in your blood as well.

You are the daughter of a King. And no matter what you do, your status will never change.

I have chosen you and I have a plan for your life.
I will not forget you and will be with you always.
I have engraved you in the palm of my hands.

Rest in the knowledge of who you are in me.
Nothing else will ever be enough.
You are my daughter and I love you!"

Share Your Thoughts

What are your comments and thoughts? Could you relate at all to this poem? Do you have your own story of finding your identity and self esteem?

Let us know what you think! Share your opinion and read what others have to say here:

http://Share.TrueBeautyBook.com

Inner Beauty Tip
Let Your Inner Beauty Shine!

Because beauty is such an important topic for us girls, I want to share an inner beauty tip with you and give you the chance to share your inner beauty with others.

Most of the time, when I think of beauty, I automatically think of someone's outer beauty. How they dress, what their hair looks like, what type of make-up they wear, etc. I have to admit that inner beauty is thought about and talked about a lot less....at least for me.

I have to make a conscious effort to focus on my inner beauty. It's a lot easier for me to look in the mirror and know that I need to wash my hair than it is to look inside myself and see where I need to grow emotionally or spiritually.

But, when I take the time to do so and then offer forgiveness to someone or connect with God, it shows! I am more fun to be around and have more joy that naturally shines through my personality.

I also believe that your inner beauty can shine through the abilities, gifts and talents God has given you.

What gifts or talents do you have? Are you a writer? Maybe you write in a journal or write poetry. Are you an artist? Maybe you paint, draw, sculpt, design graphics, etc. Are you a musician? Maybe you write lyrics or compose songs? Maybe you love to sing or play an instrument.

There are countless ways that your inner beauty and the creativity God has given you can shine through.

This is my inner beauty tip...let it shine through by sharing your creativity with others. The sky's the limit. Don't hide your inner beauty....let it shine!!

Matthew 5:14-16 *"You are the light of the world. A city on a hill cannot be hidden. Neither do people light a lamp and put it under a bowl. Instead they put it on its stand, and it gives light to everyone in the house. In the same way, **let your light shine before men**, that they may see your good deeds and praise your Father in heaven."*

Share Your Thoughts

Let Your Inner Beauty Shine!

Do you have a gift or talent to share that displays your inner beauty? It can be anything...from a journal entry to a picture of your artwork to a video of a song you performed (or wrote) or a great photo you took.

Let's share and display the inner beauty God has given us!

http://Share.TrueBeautyBook.com

My Journey to Becoming One Of
God's Prized Beauties
By Julie

Because of the influences our culture has on us as youth, especially the media and our peers, it is very difficult to go through school without being concerned with what everyone else thinks about you. It's also hard to not prescribe to the one size fits all perspective when it comes to standards of beauty, popularity, and relationships. This was true for me growing up.

➔ For as long as I can remember, I was dreadfully afraid of not fitting in. Even though I had many friends from different groups, I never had a best friend. No one seemed to need me as much as I wished they would. I wasn't liked by many boys.

➔ I grew up in a challenging school system where there were a lot of bullies and people were quickly labeled. There were a lot of cliques. I always seemed to enjoy the social environment, being friends with almost everyone, but deep down I felt unloved by all socially.

➔ I was always fearful of confrontation and internalized these feelings. I felt paralyzed when my family members fought with each other and with me. I tried to keep the peace in our household, sometimes by giving in and apologizing or taking the blame for things I didn't even do.

➔ I never thought I was pretty. Or thin. Or anything special on the outside. I knew I was worthy on the inside, but that *wasn't enough* because I was completely insecure with my appearance, thinking it wasn't up to the world's standards of worth.

➔ I started caring much more about how I was perceived by others than how I perceived myself.

54

→ I thought I was a victim because I had a lot of physical conditions, including chronic pain, that made me miss out things growing up and made me feel like I was different than my peers, fighting an invisible and lonely illness no one understood.

→ I gave in to stress in almost all areas of my life.

I came out of high school with a lot of bitterness, but it wasn't until after college that I began to realize how much it affected my choices and beliefs. I was prone to being influenced by those directly around me, and the reality is, during college a lot of us are still facing an identity crisis, and we tend to rub off on each other. During this time, because of some close peer interactions and the effect the media's portray of health was having on me, I started paying attention to things like healthy eating.

Because this obsession with healthy eating satisfied me temporarily, and was a way I thought I had finally reached a mark of self-discipline and worthiness, it was easy to slide into destructive eating habits and disordered thinking.

I'm convinced that Satan tries to deceive young girls where they are most fragile. For me, this was with health. Issues of health and wellbeing were always close to my heart, as I'd suffered from debilitating chronic pain in much of my upper body for as long as I could remember. I longed to feel well and "normal" and I believe that as a way to numb the pain I felt, I tried to control any aspects of my health that I could, through "better" eating habits, more exercising, and following many of the prescribed techniques magazines give for how to be happy.

Do you know how many times I've wanted to hit the erase button on all of the sin I fell into?

Now, I don't believe God wants to hit the erase button on me or anyone. He wants to the use the experiences we've gone through to shape us into someone who learns that apart from Him, we can do nothing (*John 15:5*).

This leads me back to Christ. I grew up in a Christian home, but it wasn't for many years that my faith became my own and I began to actually etch God's truths into my heart, placing my identity more firmly in Him. When I finally realized what God's love for me meant, there was nothing left for me to do but repent of my sinful ways and unpeel all the layers of defenses I'd built up over the years.

What I didn't realize was how dangerous it could be to become so obsessed with health, to the point where it really skewed my perception of body image. It wasn't until about a year after college when I finally started realizing what these habits were doing to me: controlling my life and seeping joy out of me.

It would not help to place blame elsewhere; I needed to own up to those things. What helped me do this was to realize that God knew the feelings in my heart, and I couldn't hide from him. In Jeremiah 16, we learn that the first step of repentance (experiencing sorrow for and seeking change for wrongs), is to acknowledge that God knows about our sin. I had to release what was holding me back from a living a more full life, inhibiting me from truly loving myself and others, and even God, the way I needed to.

To do this, I had to look at where I'd been placing my influence. I was constantly trying to reach a level of perfection that was unattainable and not part of God's plan for any of us. He wants us to be who we are, as He knit us each perfectly the way He wants us to be.

I had to realize that some aspects of who I was and also trials I went through were part of God's plan for who I was and maybe it was that way to bring me closer to Him.

It was then that I became convicted to change a lot of my behavioral patterns that had taken hold of me, especially the ways I tried to control my eating patterns and fixation on good health.

Because of all the patterns I had entered into, it was an extremely difficult process to change. Some days, I wanted to give up, but I knew that through His son, God had sacrificed so much that my sins could be washed away. Because of that, I knew it was possible to get through it all.

Day-by-day grace. That's how I got through. And continue to get through, I couldn't worry about the next day, because one day at a time was hard enough. Eventually, my absorbing thoughts controlling my eating started to diminish. Little specks of joy that I didn't think I'd ever feel again came back into my life, this time with an overflowing sense of freedom that I'd never felt before.

It was in these times that I truly learned that God's truth had meaning in my life. I began to rely on God's word to get me through tough times, as well as constant support from the godly people He placed into my life to be His hands and feet and comfort me when I needed it most.

I allowed my internal struggle to be verbalized and also allowed myself to feel emotions that had been pent up for so long. Through this process of letting go of the power all my obsessions and false idols were having on me, I was able to get healed in more ways than I could have imagined.

God healed me from the inside out, allowing me to want to get help for things that were wrong with my body, and He provided a path to do that. Jeremiah 16:19 says, "If you repent, I will restore you that you may serve me." With the physical pain I'd always had, I wondered what it would be like to truly be able to serve Him if I could just have greater energy and without distracting ailments. Surprisingly, what I've found out recently is that if my heart is hungry to serve Him, He allows me to serve, and won't let physical pain stand in the way.

I believe that whatever struggles we go through in the flesh and in our thought patterns can be renewed, and God can bring all of us, body, mind, and spirit together again, showing us that He made all of us to work as one for His glory. All my life I have wanted to be free of health issues, I have wanted a different body, but now, thanks to God, that feeling is gone.

I've had an enormous peace that God knows what He's doing with me, and He has made no mistake with me or any other girl who cries out to Him, wondering why she has to feel different. We are different, and God wants us to be. We are the only one of us that will ever be, so it's important to try and accept and even relish in that thought.

Share Your Thoughts

What is your story? How has God been working in your life lately? It could be something big or something little. Share your opinion and read what others have to say here:

http://Share.TrueBeautyBook.com

Part Two

Your Fashion Choices

Fashion Tip
My Edition of
"What Not To Wear"

There are many people giving out their advice on the latest fashion tip....helping you "dress to impress." I have to admit that for most of my life I have enjoyed shopping for new clothes and putting cute outfits together. For those of us that enjoy shopping, it's fun isn't it? The rush of buying something new and having the satisfaction of "creating the look."

Some of you are like me in that you tend to trust in your beauty (Ezekiel 16:15). It makes you feel good to be the best dressed in the room.   But, for others, you avoid the mall like the plague and are content wearing t-shirts and jeans every day.

There are Many Differing Opinions, But What is God's Advice and Fashion Tip for our Culture Today?

WWJD - "What Would Jesus Do?"

On the same line have you ever thought of WWJD as "What Wouldn't Jesus Do?" Just as you might not eat a certain type of food because you know it will make you sick or give you heartburn, I believe there are certain fashion choices that can lead to "spiritual heartburn." There may be certain things Jesus asks us to avoid because he knows the heartache it will bring. I know this from personal experience.

The good news is that we are not without God's help when it comes to our fashion and clothing choices.

2 Peter 1:3 says, "His divine power has given us _everything we need_ for life and godliness through our knowledge of him who called us by his own glory and goodness."

Notice it says _everything_. It doesn't say "except for this latest generation -- they really have me stumped in this area of fashion."

I believe we can apply God's word and find the answers we need for _everything_...even our clothing and fashion choices. Some of you may be tuning me out right now, but stick with me so you can see for yourself.

Let's think about this question for a moment - what influences you the most in regards to the clothes you buy and wear?

It could be a number of things:

- Your friends
- The media (TV, magazines, movies, billboards, etc)
- Your parents
- Your boyfriend (or husband if you are married)
- God

In what order would you rate those influences in your life?

Confession Time

Well, this is confession time for me. I have to admit that there was a time in my life when I was primarily influenced in my clothing choices by the media. I spent a lot of time watching shows like "What Not to Wear," "How Do I Look?," "Extreme

Makeover," etc. I also scanned the latest magazines any chance I could get to gain a few more fashion tips.

As I began to become *saturated* by the influence of media in the area of fashion, my clothing style gradually began to change. Even though I would never have admitted it, what I was trying to achieve by the way I dressed was the "sexy look" that is advertised everywhere. I like to think about it as if I was changing my "PR campaign" and the way I "advertised" myself. And in doing so, I slowly began to compromise in how I dressed in order to get the attention I wanted and to feel good about myself.

Yet, I was a Christian and had been a Christian for years. Satan knew he couldn't get me to immediately start to dress like Brittney Spears and many of the pop idols today. But, if the change was gradual, he knew it would be easier for me to fall for it.

And I did.

That's how our enemy, Satan, often works. He plays us like a video game, trying to win *one level at a time*. Once he wins the first level then he moves on to the second and so forth. Compromising in the way you dress can be a slippery slope that will eventually impact your actions - the way you flirt with guys and your sexual choices.

For me, my clothes gradually became tighter, showing off my figure, and the shirts became lower.

I was not oblivious; I knew the impact my clothing choices were having. I could tell you exactly which outfits in my closet would get me the most attention from the guys I was around. Deep down I knew...and I imagine you do too.

I Came To My Senses

I'm so thankful that God got my attention. It's as if, like the prodigal son, I came to my senses (Luke 15:17) and woke up to the reality of my poor clothing choices as just one outward sign of my slowly dying spiritual life.

At that time, I read a book called "Every Woman's Battle" by Shannon Etheridge and felt like she was writing the book about me. I looked over my shoulder wondering if she had been peeking inside my life as she was writing this book.

For myself and many girls and women today, there is a reason we dress the way we do.

First of all, we have a God given desire to look beautiful. That is a good thing. God created us beautiful and His creation wasn't complete until He created woman. Think about that the next time you see a beautiful sunset or mountain range. God's creation wasn't complete without you!!

Have you noticed that there is power in our beauty? God created it to be this way.

"Modesty is the source of this delicate yet formidable power, making it a power in and of itself. It's delicate because it can be so innocently given away without your even knowing it. It's formidable - or difficult to deal with or control - because once you've mastered it, no man will be given access to the full secrets behind your allure until you so desire." [30]

--Dannah Gresh

I'm sure you've noticed the many differences between how guys and girls respond to relationships. There have been entire books written about this. But to summarize, guys are primarily visual and attracted to what they see, while girls are primarily emotional and long to be deeply loved and accepted.

So, how does this relate to God's advice about our fashion choices?

Well, I realized that my PR campaign had changed. And if I continued advertising in this same way, I would eventually make choices I would regret. Choices that would hurt both God and my husband.

Although I had been a Christian for a long time, no one really taught me God's principles in this area. So, I began to ask God for His help in my clothing choices and here is some of the advice I was given.

#1 - I Was Drinking From a Broken Cup

This is the image I got regarding my life:

I was holding a cup and trying to fill it up each day with water. I would first go to my husband and when he showed me love or affirmation, he poured a little water in my cup. Then, I would be at work and if my boss was pleased with my work, he would put a little water in my cup as well. When I would go shopping, the thrill of getting a bargain and something new would also put some water in my cup. Later when I talked to my family and friends on the phone, they would fill up my cup some too.

But, there was a problem.

The "water" in my cup didn't satisfy. I had to keep going back for more and more to satisfy my thirst, the emptiness inside. This was because I was drinking from a broken cup.

Have you ever felt this way? For you, it could be that food, drugs, shopping, sex, flirting, talking or texting on your cell phone, or a number of other things temporarily fill your cup. And it's easy for these things to become addictions because we have to keep going back to them again and again in order to feel good.

In Jeremiah 2:13, God describes what happened to me. "My people have committed two sins: They have forsaken me, the spring of living water, and have dug their own cisterns, broken cisterns that cannot hold water."

I had forsaken God, my source of living water that would completely satisfy me and had settled for my broken cistern or what I call my broken cup.

Jeremiah 17:5-8 contrasts living a life trusting in yourself or human strength versus trusting in God.

"This is what the Lord says: Cursed is the one who trusts in man, who depends on flesh for his strength and whose heart turns away from the Lord. He will be like a bush in the wastelands; he will not see prosperity when it comes. He will dwell in the parched places of the desert, in a salt land where no one lives.

But blessed is the man who trusts in the Lord, whose confidence is in him. He will be like a tree planted by the water that sends out its roots by the stream. It does not fear when heat comes; its leaves are always green. It has no worries in a year of drought and never fails to bear fruit."

My first step, like the woman at the well in John 4, was to exchange my broken cup for God's living water.

When I did this, it was as if instead of drinking a drop here or there, I was now drinking out of a fire hydrant hose with more water than I could ever imagine!

#2 - I Realized I was Walking as a "Candle Among Gunpowder"

"You must not lay a stumbling block in their way, nor blow up the fire of their lust...You must walk among sinful persons, as you could do with a candle among straw or gunpowder, or else you may see the flame which you did not foresee, when it is too late to quench."   --Richard Baxter

I became very convicted when I read Jesus' words in Luke 17:1-3 and thought about how it relates to how I dress -- possibly creating lust in guys. It says, "Things that cause people to sin are bound to come, but *woe to that person through whom they come.* It would be better for (her) to be thrown into the sea with a millstone tied around (her) neck than for (her) to cause one of these little ones to sin. So watch yourselves."

Did you know that Jesus said in Matthew 5:28 that "anyone who looks at a woman lustfully has already committed adultery with her in his heart"?

Now I'm not saying the blame goes only to the girls here. The guys also have a responsibility for their thought lives. But, God showed me that I do have a responsibility to dress in a way that is honoring to God and not tempting guys to lust.

I will give you some general ideas below, but there are no set "modesty rules." Each person needs to talk with God about this and decide what standards He is asking you to live by.

66

"Imagine how fulfilling it will be if you save it all...every moment of passion, every bared curve, every suggestive glance! Imagine the powerful "intoxication" you'll create for the man of your dreams if you keep the deepest secrets of your beauty just for him." [31]   --Dannah Gresh

#3 - I Was Stealing What Belonged to Someone Else

Would you go to a girlfriend's house and steal her favorite CD, outfit or even her dog? Most of us would never even think of doing such a thing. I would never call myself a thief. But, I was. I was stealing guy's emotional and sexual energy that belonged only to their wives or future wives.

I get very angry when I think of other girls "taking" my husband's emotional and sexual energy that doesn't belong to them -- it belongs to me. Then, I end up with the leftovers. And yet, I was guilty of taking other men's emotional and sexual energy by the way I dressed and interacted with them.

Your future husband is out there somewhere right now. How do you want the girls around him to treat him? Do you want them to dress and act in ways that tempt him to lust and then possibly act on that lust? It's something for each of us to consider.

#4 - The Time and Money Spent Achieving "The Look"

How long would you estimate it takes you to get ready in the mornings? Remember that on average women spend 2.5 years of their life washing, styling, cutting, coloring, crimping and straightening their hair at home and in the salon. And that's just the time spent on our hair!

What about the time you spend shopping? I used to spend hours and hours every week shopping for the latest fashions at bargain prices. I didn't spend a ton of money, but I was spending a lot of my time. And yet I would say that I didn't have time for God.

Comparing and contrasting the world's outer beauty to inner beauty...

<u>Outer Beauty</u>:

- Costs me time to get ready in the morning and to go shopping
- Costs me money for make-up, clothes, etc.
- Fades with time
- Common – fairly easy to obtain, there is always someone more attractive than me
- Focus is on myself – selfish
- Others may envy me and feel inferior
- Vanity is a sin (as well as pride, greed, seduction, materialism)
- It's easy to trust in my beauty instead of God (Ezekiel 16:13-15)
- Draws the attention of men and feeds into my other struggles
- Never satisfies (broken cup) "Everyone who drinks this water will be thirsty again (John 4:13-14)

<u>Inner Beauty</u>:

- Costs me time to spend with God
- Costs nothing financially but will possibly cost me the approval of the world
- Unfading

- Rare – difficult to obtain (in that you have to face the pain in your life and receive healing)
- Focus is on God
- Others are drawn to me
- It is great worth in God's sight.
- Completely satisfies, drink the living water Jesus gives and you will never thirst. A spring of water welling up to eternal life.

Is it Possible...

...to Dress Trendy Without Dressing Trashy? To Be Modern, Yet Modest?

Yes!!

As God began convicting my heart, I decided to go through my closet. I'm sorry to say that some of my favorite outfits had to go. This was a decision between me and God. No one was forcing me to get rid of anything; I just knew in my heart that I needed to.

Boy, did I ever have a big stack of clothes to get rid of! Anything I wasn't sure about, I modeled for my husband and had him make the final verdict (since he knows how guys think).

I needed to start thinking differently when I was shopping for clothes. I soon found a "secret weapon" to help make today's trendy clothes acceptable for those of us walking with God and in purity.

Guess what it is?

The Secret Weapon...

 What is the secret weapon? A simple tank top t-shirt.

How can this be used as your secret weapon to transform your trendy clothes? Well, it's all about layering. You wear it underneath your other shirts.

Here are a few examples of the way I use mine:

1. When my shirt is too low in front
2. When my shirt raises up and shows my stomach when I lift my arms overhead
3. When my button up shirt gaps and shows my bra
4. When my waist line is lower than the bottom of my shirt

I tell you what, I have really used this "secret weapon" a lot. I've gotten to the point where I need to buy more because it seems like the one I want to wear is in the laundry. They come in different colors, but the one I use the most is the white one. It may take a little hunting to find the ones that will work best (not too low in the front, the right colors, etc.) but it's been worth it for me!

Now, I won't lie to you. It does take me longer to find trendy clothes that fit my standards. But, it's not impossible.

Girls, we don't have to dress in big, ugly, baggy clothes in order to "honor God with our bodies." I Corinthians 6:19-20

How Are You Advertising Your Body?

Chapter Ten

Did you know that each one of us is running a PR campaign by the way we "advertise" our bodies? For those of you wondering, PR stands for Public Relations and is the way we present ourselves to others by the way we dress. We live in a culture that encourages girls to advertise in a "sexy" way in order to attract the attention of guys. Pop stars like Brittney Spears, Jessica Simpson, Paris Hilton, and others often encourage this type of "advertising."

In order to help us understand the impact of our PR campaign, I want to share this illustration with you. However, realize this illustration is not complete. It is just one way to get us to rethink how we advertise our bodies.

Ford Truck?

My husband and I used to have a Ford Ranger Truck. It was a great vehicle. But, overall, a Ford truck is a fairly economical vehicle, right? Therefore, for this illustration, let's say it is in the *"cheaper car market."* There are many other brands in this *"cheaper car market."*

Can you name some?

→ What about....Chevy, Mazda, Dodge, Nissan, Mitsubishi, Toyota, and the list could go on and on.

71

You get the idea, right?

Well, because there are so many other vehicles in this *"cheaper car market"* competing for the same buyers, the Ford truck ___has___ to advertise. Therefore, you'll see advertisements in the newspapers, radio ads and TV commercials.

You might see an ad like this, "Blowout Prices on Ford Trucks at Bob's Corner Lot. Lowest Prices of the Year - Hurry in Today!"

Just like a Ford truck ___has___ to advertise, you may feel the pressure to "advertise" your bodies in order to attract certain guys and compete against all the other pretty girls in the *"cheap car market."*

However, realize that you'll attract a certain type of buyer by the way you advertise. In this example, we'll call them the *"cheap car buyers."* These *"cheap car buyers"* are those boys who are interested in looking under the hood, taking you for a test drive and then eventually trading you in for a newer model.

Is that all there is? The cheap car market?

Sometimes it may seem like there is only one option. But, I'm here to tell you that there is another option.

Do you recognize this car name?

Lamborghini.

What is a Lamborghini? Well, it's a car that costs up to half a million dollars. That's a lot of money!

72

For this illustration, we'll say it belongs in the *"classy car market,"* including other cars like the Ferrari and Rolls Royce.

Have you ever seen an advertisement in your local newspaper for a Lamborghini? Probably not. And why not?

Think about it...if you have enough money to buy a Lamborghini, you probably know where to find one. Therefore, a Lamborghini doesn't need to advertise to convince you to buy it. You buy it because you have enough money and have chosen the Lamborghini over all the other cars you could have bought instead.

Just like a Lamborghini, if you are in the *"classy car market"* you won't feel the need to advertise your body to all the potential buyers. You may have to wait a while for that *"classy car buyer,"* but when the right one comes along, you'll be glad you waited. Have you ever seen how *"classy car buyers"* treat their cars? They treat them with respect, keeping them in the garage, washed and waxed...and usually own them for a lifetime.

Which type of buyer do you want to attract?

I think deep down most of us want to attract a guy that loves us for who we are and treats us with the utmost respect. We want to attract someone who has chosen us over all the other girls in the world and wants to be with us for a lifetime - in a committed relationship, called marriage.

How Will You Choose to Advertise? What Type of PR Campaign are you Running?

It's time to look at yourself and decide how you have been advertising your body.

Are you advertising in the *"cheap car market,"* like a Ford, to attract the *"cheap car buyers"* or in the *"classy car market,"* like a Lamborghini, to the *"classy car buyers?"*

Are you compromising your standards and allowing guys to look under the hood and take a test drive in order to be in a relationship <u>now</u>? Or are you waiting patiently for that *"classy car buyer"* who will cherish you and treat you with respect?

Be a Lamborghini.

I encourage you to be a Lamborghini. Even if you've been advertising in the *"cheap car market,"* like I did, it's never too late to change.

How do you want to be treated?

I've never seen a Lamborghini in a junk yard. And yet I've see hundreds of Ford trucks. Why? My guess is that the *"classy car buyers"* take care of the Lamborghinis while the Ford trucks are used, abused and then discarded for the latest model. How do you want to be treated?

Let's choose to be treasures and not targets!

 Share Your Thoughts

How do you dress in a way that honors God? Share your fashion secrets and ideas here:

http://Fashion.TrueBeautyBook.com

There Are No Set "Modesty Rules"

What?!? Did you read that right? Yes! I want to make sure you understand I'm not trying to shove "101 modesty rules" down your throat. I realize that every girl's body is different and may look differently in the same clothes. *So, what applies to me, may not apply to you.* Plus, modesty comes from the heart, so this is something between you and God.

A Few of My Modesty Tips...

These are only tips and not rules. But, they can get you started in the right direction. So, let's do a quick modesty check from head to toe.

1. **Is the neckline of my shirt too low?** I try to make sure I can put my palm between the top of my bra and the top of my neckline.
   <u>Solution</u>: Wear a tank top underneath your shirt.

2. **When I lean over does my shirt gap?**
   <u>Solution</u>: Use double sided tape to hold your neckline in place or wear a tank top underneath your shirt.

3. **Are my bra straps showing?**
   <u>Solution</u>: Pin your straps in place or layer a shirt over top.

4. **Is my shirt too tight?**
   <u>Solution</u>: Layer another shirt or jacket over top, sometimes I buy a bigger size than normal.

5. **Does my belly show when I lift my hands overhead?**
   <u>Solution</u>: Wear a tank top underneath your shirt

6. **Can you see my underwear when I lean over?**
   <u>Solution</u>: Wear a tank top underneath your shirt tucked in

7. **Are my pants or skirts too tight? Does my panty line show through?**
   <u>Solution</u>: Wear a longer shirt untucked that covers your hips or wear looser pants and skirts.

8. **Is my skirt or shorts too short?** *Note* sit down and look in front of a mirror to check.
   <u>Solution</u>: Wear board shorts or Capri's or long skirts

My Solution for Tight Pants?

I used to think the only thing I needed to be concerned about regarding *the waist down* was wearing skirts or shorts too short. But, then I became convicted that when I was buying pants, I was concerned with how "cute" my butt looked.

I started to notice that if I was standing behind a group of people and the girls were wearing tight pants, my eyes automatically went to their butt. I began to wonder if that is what happened to other people when they looked at me from behind. I came to the conclusion that they did. And I decided it was in my best interests to avoid wearing jeans or pants that are too tight or form fitting. Why? It was one more decision I was making to honor God with my body.

My solution? Cute skirts, long shirts, long sweaters, athletic pants that aren't as tight, etc.

Long Sweaters

Fun Skirts

You have to decide for yourself what your modesty standards will be...that's between you and God.

Get more modesty tips at:
http://Fashion.TrueBeautyBook.com

My Journey to Find Modest Swimwear

The Swimsuit Dilemma

Have you found it difficult to find modest swimwear? Me too! Here's a little about my journey...

I have to admit that as God began to get a hold of my heart in the area of fashion and modesty, I began to think differently. As I began to think differently, I began to question things I had always just accepted. Things I had just accepted as "normal." One of the things I began to question was our typical American swimsuit.

Beginning to Question My Swimsuit Standards

Questions like these began to enter my mind...

- What is the history of swimsuits? Have we always worn revealing suits like we do today or did they previously wear modest swimwear?
- Why am I willing to lower my standards regarding modesty for swimwear when I have willingly made changes in the rest of my wardrobe?
- What does God think of my choice of swimwear? Am I pleasing Him in this area?

These are not easy questions with easy answers. To be honest, I tried to ignore the issue of modest swimwear at first. I don't swim very often, so I just didn't take the time to decide how I would handle it.

Until I got this e-mail...

Hi Shelley!

I am a new reader of your site, and I have to say that it is wonderful! It has helped me so much with my relationship with God and my family. My parents have never stressed the importance of being modest, and don't really have a close relationship with God, so you (unknowingly) have been helping me along.

I'm just 14 years old and in need of help. Personally, I don't really have anyone to go to with this question..... my mother doesn't understand how I'm feeling no matter how I phrase it. I'm struggling with modesty. With a school focused on looking "hott" when we're JUST 14, there's a lot of pressure.

With bathing suit season coming up, and skimpy less-than-lingerie bikinis EVERYWHERE, I'm afraid I may cave into the temptation and buy one.

What's your view on modest swimwear? Bikinis? Halters? One pieces?

I realized when I received this e-mail it was finally time to tackle this difficult question...what would be my stand on modest swimwear? I began to pray and ask God for His wisdom because I knew I didn't have the answers on my own.

The History of Swimwear

As I began researching the history of swimwear, I found it interesting that it wasn't until the 1920's that women began wearing the type of swimsuit that we now wear today. And at that time, it was still strictly a one-piece bathing suit. It wasn't until 1946 that the bikini was "re-invented" by two Frenchmen, Jacques Heim and Louis Reard. Today, most women wear either a one piece, a tankini or a bikini...some more revealing than others.

Check out a few pictures of swimwear from the past...

So, my first question was answered. Have we always worn revealing suits like we do today? No. They used to wear more modest swimwear, it has just been in the last 60 years that bikini's were "re-invented."

My Double Standards, Feeling Like a Hypocrite

The more I thought about my swimsuit choices, the more I began to feel like a hypocrite. Why, you ask? Well, God had convicted me of my fashion choices and I was starting to dress differently. You see, I decided that I could dress trendy and cute as long as I didn't compromise my modesty standards.

But it seemed like my swimsuit choices broke all my modesty standards.

I started thinking....there's no way I would walk around on the street by strangers, in my bra and underwear, so why would I feel comfortable at the beach in a bikini (which is very similar to a bra and underwear) walking by strangers?

Or I wouldn't choose to wear a really tight tank top and underwear to a friend's house to hang out, so why do I feel okay about wearing my tankini when hanging out by the pool?

I started to realize that I would have to change my swimsuit choices, but to be honest, I didn't want to. It didn't seem like anyone else, even other Christians, were willing to stand out and be different. It seemed like everyone I knew gave in to the culture and wore the typical swimsuit. It seemed like the only "modest" swimwear choice was a one piece or tankini that wasn't too low cut on the top and wasn't cut too high on the bottom.

Was that really the only modest swimwear choice? Or am I just afraid of standing out and being different? I have to be honest, I was afraid to be different. It's something I've struggled with my whole life....choosing to please people rather than God. Wanting to fit in and be accepted by people and not "rock the boat." It's easier, or so it seems.

What does God think of my choice of swimwear? Am I pleasing Him in this area?

I had to make a decision. Would I choose to please people or choose to please God. What does God think of my current swimwear choices?

I have to admit that there is not a verse in the bible that mentions the words "swimsuit" "bathing suit" "modest swimwear" or "bikini." But, God does give us some of His thoughts about modesty and sexuality.

- I Corinthians 6:19-20 says, "Do you not know that your body is a temple of the Holy Spirit, who is in you, whom you have received from God? You are not your own; you were bought at a price. Therefore *honor God with your body*."
- Ephesians 5:3 says, "But among you *there must not be even a hint of sexual immorality*, or of any kind of impurity, or of greed, because these are improper for God's holy people."
- Matthew 5:28 says, "But I tell you that anyone who looks at a woman lustfully has already committed adultery with her in his heart."
- Luke 17:1-3 says, "Jesus said to his disciples: "Things that cause people to sin are bound to come, *but woe to that person through whom they come.* It would be better for (her) to be thrown into the sea with a millstone tied around (her) neck than for (her) to cause one of these little ones to sin. So watch yourselves."

God asks us to honor Him with our bodies. For me, I began to realize that I was not honoring God with my body in my swimsuit choices....instead I was compromising my standards and flaunting my beauty before others, possibly causing others to sin by lusting after my body.

Decision Time Regarding Modest Swimwear

I now felt convicted that I didn't want to continue wearing the same tankini that I've worn for the last couple of years.

Even though it is considered fairly modest swimwear – according to what is available these days. So, if I'm not going to wear the tankini, what am I going to wear?

I started searching the internet for "modest swimsuits" to see what was out there. I was pretty disappointed because there is really not much available. There are a few options, but for the most part, I would have to compromise my standards of fashion in order to be modest. I wondered...is it really possible to find modest swimwear that would still be trendy and cute? So my search began.

A Look At Surfers Attire...Board Shorts and Rash Guards

Several of the websites I visited discussed the option of wearing board shorts and rash guard shirts as a modest alternative to the traditional swimsuit. Women surfers usually wear this type of outfit to protect their skin from the sun and to be more functional....so their swimsuit doesn't fall off as they are fighting the waves.

So, I thought, if surfers wear something like this, why not me? I don't think it would be a perfect solution for modest swimwear, but it could possibly work.

My First Attempt at a Modest Swimsuit

First I looked up board shorts and rash guards online. I'll warn you that they tend to be expensive. But, if you look on eBay, you may run across some that will work for you.

My next stop was the mall. I went a couple weeks before summer clothes were released and there was nothing anywhere that would work for me.

I waited a couple weeks and then found a cute pair of board shorts at Wal-Mart for under $15. I thought that was a pretty good deal. I then looked for a shirt I could wear to match the shorts. I figured I would be wearing a sports bra underneath it, but wanted something made out of material that would dry fast.

I found a shirt at Kohl's on sale that is 90% nylon and 10% spandex which is the same material you'll find in a typical swimsuit. I decided to wear a tight fitting tank top underneath (80% nylon, 20% spandex) and found the tank top in the lingerie section because it's a type of shape wear that you can wear under clothes. Since my shirt is white, I needed to make sure that my sports bra didn't show through. Also, if the shirt comes up while I'm swimming it won't show anything since I have the other tank top underneath. All in all, I spent about $40 for this option.

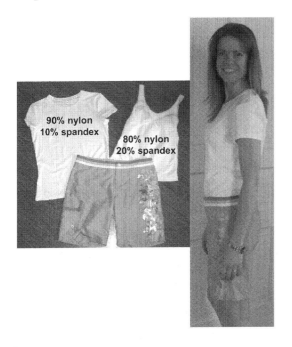

Let's Get Creative

Wearing board shorts and a shirt is not the only modest swimwear option. But, it's the option I've chosen for me right now. What about you? What other ways can you think of to help make your swimsuit choices pleasing to God and honor Him with your body?

- What about wearing a tankini with a swim skirt overtop.
- Or maybe you know someone who sews or you can sew yourself and can design your own modest swimsuits! Maybe you could design a pair of swim shorts or swim skirt.
- Or what if you take what you already have and modify it to be more modest?

I think the most important part is to realize you do have options. Realize that you're not alone in this dilemma and that many other girls struggle to find an option for modest swimwear.

What Do You Think About Modest Swimwear? This tends to be a controversial topic, even amongst Christians. What do you think? Are you comfortable wearing a bikini? What are some ways you think we can address this issue? Let us know what you think at:

http://Share.TrueBeautyBook.com

Part Three

Sex and Dating

To Date or Not To Date?

I have to admit that I'm not a dating or relationship expert. But, when I look back on my dating habits before getting married, I will admit that I have many regrets. Why? Well, let me tell you a little more of my story and what I learned.

How it All Began

You see, I grew up in a Christian home. I learned that I should "save sex for marriage" and that I should "only date Christian guys." However, what I was taught about dating was very limited and my main influences came from my friends and the media. I ended up adapting a self-centered approach to romance and dating early on.

My parents told me I wasn't allowed to date until I was sixteen. For some reason, that tends to be the "magical age" when we are suddenly ready and mature enough to date. However, my sophomore year, a senior guy started pursuing me and I convinced my parents to allow me to start dating earlier…about 6 months before I turned sixteen.

I enjoyed the attention my boyfriend gave me. In a selfish way, I saw my relationship with him as a way to feel good about myself. He made me feel special, he listened to me and I felt loved by him. It felt good that he had chosen me over all the other girls in the school to be his girlfriend.

Because he had a car, dating him opened up a whole new world of independence for me. We spent a lot of time together that year. I remember one night early on in our relationship; he pressured me to have sex with him. I was very strong in my conviction that I would save sex for marriage and said, "No." He said he would respect that boundary...and he did keep his word. We never had sexual intercourse. However, even though we didn't cross the line and have intercourse, we went very close to the edge, a place I have come to regret. I ended up breaking up with my boyfriend when he went away to college that next year, but he took a piece of my heart with him.

Looking for Love in All the Wrong Places

They say hind sight is "20/20." Looking back on my dating experiences, I realize some of my life circumstances set the stage for me to see guys in a distorted way...in a selfish way, for what I could get out of the relationship.

Unlike some of you, I had a dad that was present in my life. He came to all my games and activities and was a good financial provider for our family. However, his job as the pastor of our church often took much of his time and emotional energy.

Even though he was a good provider in many ways, he didn't connect with me on a deeper emotional level. He left that to my mom. He admits that he didn't truly know how to express his feelings until he was an adult. So, in some ways, I left childhood feeling emotionally neglected by my dad. I _knew_ he loved me, but deep down I still didn't _feel_ loved by him. Instead, I felt emptiness inside, a longing to be loved.

Then, just as I was getting interested in boys, a popular guy in our school used me for what he wanted sexually and then never talked to me again. I felt rejected and hurt. As an adult, I realize that he stole something very precious from me...my innocence.

Using Guys to Feel Good About Myself

Through this experience, my eyes were opened to realize the power I held as a female to influence guys. And I began to use this power to my advantage. I realized that I could gain guys' attention by how I dressed and interacted with them. Even though I wasn't having sex with these guys, I still knew how to allure them with my eyes, my smile and my body.

Some of my friends would joke with me in college that I knew how to "attract all the guys." I now regret those years of self-centered relationships. I am ashamed to say that I "attracted the guys" because I had learned how to be a "flirt." It was something I had control over and used to feel good about myself.

Isaiah 3:16 (AMP) explains it pretty well, *"the daughters of Zion are haughty and walk with outstretched necks and with **undisciplined (flirtatious and alluring) eyes**."*

Therefore, since I had this longing to be loved and knew how to attract a guy's attention, I saw guys as one way to _fill_ the emptiness I _felt_ on the inside.

It was purely selfish.

I wasn't thinking of their best interests, but only mine. Just like many other girls, I played the games and broke many hearts.

88

Even after I committed my life to Christ, I still didn't fully surrender this area of romance and dating to Him. Because of this, I carried some of those habits I had developed into my marriage. Not good! God finally got my attention after some really hard years and many mistakes, almost costing me my marriage.

Jesus Rescued Me

I am thankful to say that Jesus rescued me from the path of destruction I was headed down. You see, I was living a self-centered life. Instead of allowing God to help me forgive those who hurt me, heal my past hurts, and fill me completely with His love, I was trying to do things my own way in this area of relating to guys.

I realized that I needed to surrender this area of my life and allow God to change my thoughts and my actions. God began to transform me and the way I interacted with guys. He began to convict me in many areas, including modesty and flirting, and began to change me from the inside out.

Instead of living for myself and what makes me feel good, I am now a new creation and am to live for Christ.

In 2 Corinthians 5:14-15 Paul writes,
*"For Christ's love compels us, because we are convinced that one died for all, and therefore all died. And he died for all, that those who live **should no longer live for themselves but for him** who died for them and was raised again."*

2 Corinthians 5:17 says,
"Therefore, if anyone is in Christ, he is a new creation; the old has gone, the new has come!"

Jesus promises to fill me completely with His love. I don't need to go searching for it in relationships with guys.

Ephesians 3:16-19 says, *"I pray that out of his glorious riches he (Jesus) may strengthen you with power through his Spirit in your inner being, so that Christ may dwell in your hearts through faith. And I pray that you, being rooted and established in love, may have power, together with all the saints, **to grasp how wide and long and high and deep is the love of Christ, and to know this love that surpasses knowledge—**that you may be filled to the measure of all the fullness of God.*"

The amplified version says to be "flooded with God Himself."

The Self-Centered Dating Game

How about you? Have you gotten caught up in this self-centered dating game? Our culture encourages a string of short term relationships…looking for intimacy without commitment. I know I got caught up in it.

Intimacy without Commitment?

What this teaches us is intimacy without commitment and sets us up to continue in this cycle even after we're married. We learn how to have one short term relationship after another while dating. Therefore, when things get tough in marriage, we may be more willing to settle for divorce instead of staying committed to our spouse, "for better or worse."

When we have a relationship with God, then we will desire to please Him in all areas of our lives, including this area of dating and relationships. What is God's standard?

His standard for us is intimacy within a committed relationship called marriage.

As Joshua Harris says in his book, I Kissed Dating Goodbye,

> "An intimate relationship is a beautiful experience that God wants us to enjoy. After all, He stated that it wasn't good for man to be alone and created the woman to perfectly complement him and help him (Genesis 2:18). But God has made the fulfillment of intimacy a by-product of commitment based love. If we want to experience the goodness of His plan, we need to reconnect the pursuit of intimacy with the pursuit of commitment. This is what I call the Little Relationship Principle: *The joy of intimacy is the reward of commitment.*"[32]

Time to Kiss Dating Good-bye?

This might sound radical to you, but I want to encourage you to consider avoiding romantic, one-on-one relationships until marriage. Not that you won't have any opposite sex relationships, but *appropriate* friendships with guys. Not giving too much of your heart or asking for their exclusive affections unless you are ready to consider marriage. Some might call this courtship.

Otherwise, like I did, it's easy to take your focus off of God and use that guy to meet your short term needs…not thinking about the long term effects for both of you!

Imagine actually loving the guy friends in your life, not with the selfish kind of love so often demonstrated in dating, but with the kind of love God encourages. True Love.

I Corinthians 13:4-8 tells us about this kind of true love. It's not just the passionate kiss or embrace, but demonstrated in self-control, patience, etc.

Love is patient, love is kind. It does not envy, it does not boast, it is not proud. It is not rude, it is not self-seeking, it is not easily angered, it keeps no record of wrongs. Love does not delight in evil but rejoices with the truth. It always protects, always trusts, always hopes, always perseveres. Love never fails."

The Gift of Singleness and the Distraction of Boys

Before you are married, you have a gift…the "gift of singleness." It's a gift of time. This is the one season in your life that you have more extra time than any other.

How will you choose to spend your gift of time? Will you invest all of it into boys and dating or will you choose to honor God with your time and devote this season of your life to Him? Or will you get distracted and dedicate most of your time to a guy, who statistics say you will probably not marry if you are in high school?

Looking back at my high school years, I spent a lot of my time on things that don't really matter today. And a huge chunk of my time and energy went into my boyfriends. I have asked God for forgiveness and He has forgiven me, but I can never get that time back.

Instead of being immersed in boyfriends, you could spend time developing relationships with your family and your girlfriends. Maybe there is someone that needs your support or encouragement.

Or maybe you could begin using the gifts and abilities God has given you in a ministry. You could volunteer in a ministry already established, or start one of your own under the direction of trusted adults. I know some teens that have written books that have influenced their generations. God could be leading you into many different directions. All you need to do is surrender your time and then listen to where He leads you.

Instead of worrying about when you'll get a boyfriend or when you'll get married, start enjoying your "Gift of Singleness!!"

Stop and take a moment right now to pray about this area of dating and romance. If you are willing, surrender to God any current and future relationships as well as your future husband. Ask God for wisdom on how to proceed. Write down your prayer or any thoughts you have. Are you ready to "Kiss Dating Good-bye?"

_____

_____

_____

_____

_____

_____

_____

Flirting

Innocent Fun?

Most girls tend to be romantics. We love when a guy goes out of his way to set up the perfect date.

Chapter Thirteen

The flowers. The candlelight. Enjoying quality time together. His voice telling us how beautiful we look. The music.

I remember one particular date my husband set up for me on Valentine's Day. He had a trail of paper hearts leading to the basement where he had a table set up for a candlelight dinner. He doesn't cook, so it meant a lot to me that he cooked the entire meal himself. Plus, he made my favorite dessert - cheesecake!

I think I fell a little harder for him that night because I knew he cared enough to put the time into planning our time together. Flirting goes hand in hand with romance and is what we'll be talking about here.

Is all flirting innocent fun or does it lead to something more?

Does God's Word give us the "do's and don'ts" of flirting?

I looked up in my concordance in my bible and found "flirting" once. In Isaiah 3:16 it talks about women "flirting with their eyes."

However, in Song of Songs, we read an important principle we can apply to flirting and dating. This principle is repeated three times in Song of Songs. It's found in Song of Songs 2:7, 3:5 and 8:4.

In the bible, anytime something is repeated, it usually means we should pay attention because it is something pretty important.

Let's take a look at what it says....

"Daughters of Jerusalem, I charge you by the gazelles and by the does of the field; *Do not arouse or awaken love until it so desires.*"

Song of Songs is a love story. If you didn't realize romance is in the bible, it is!

We are given some good advice...."Do not awaken or arouse love until it so desires."

Think of it this way. Your sexuality is a gift to be enjoyed with one person in a committed relationship called marriage. Until that time, your sexuality is "asleep."

However, it is possible to "arouse" your sexuality earlier than marriage or outside of marriage. And once it's "aroused" or "awakened" - know this - it's really hard to convince your sexuality to go back to "sleep." Some of us know this from personal experience.

Once your sexuality is wide awake, it's hard to turn it off. It's like the proverbial slippery slope where one thing leads to another.

James 1:13-15 says, "When tempted, no one should say, 'God is tempting me.' For God cannot be tempted by evil, nor does he tempt anyone; but each one is tempted when, by his own evil desire, he is dragged away and enticed. Then, after desire has conceived, it gives birth to sin; and sin, when it is full-grown, gives birth to death."

Did you see that it all started with the temptation that then led to desire then to sin and finally to death? When we give in to sexual immorality it will eventually lead to spiritual death.

Another way to think about it is, once you get the engine running, it's hard to get the car parked again.

So how can we "arouse" or "awaken" our sexuality?

Some of us do it as we are innocently flirting and having fun. We think it's really no big deal. But, one thing does lead to another, the hormones increase and before we know it, we've done something we regret.

It's like the frog in the pot of water. If the water was boiling, the frog will immediately jump right back out and avoid its death. However, if you start with cold water and then gradually heat it up, the frog won't realize what's happening and will end up dying a slow death.

The same thing can happen to us with sexual temptation.

Hayley DiMarco talks about this in her book, "Technical Virgin, How far is too far." [33]

She talks about back rubs and tickle fights as innocent flirting that can very easily "arouse or awaken" the sexual desires within us that lead us to compromising sexually. I think she has a good point. If you don't think back rubs and tickle fights are sexual she says to ask your boyfriend these questions.

✓ *"Does he give his 82 year old grandma back rubs?*
✓ *Does he have tickle fights with his buddies?"* [34]

Most likely his answer will be "no" because they are both sexual in nature. Other things Hayley warns us to avoid are napping together and skin on skin.

All of these things put us in positions to start thinking about sex. Jesus said it wasn't just our actions on sin that counted, but also our thoughts. He's very clear about this. In Matthew 5:27-28 he says, "You have heard that it was said, 'Do not commit adultery.' But I tell you that anyone who looks at a woman lustfully has already committed adultery with her in his heart."

So what do you think? Is your flirting arousing and awakening something within you?

Something that is leading you down a sexual path you never intended to go? It's never too late to put your sexuality back to "sleep" until God brings that one person into your life for marriage. It may be difficult, but God has the power to overcome any stronghold in our lives.

Have you already compromised sexually? Remember there is forgiveness for you in God if you'll take it (Chapter 22).

Emotional Virginity

What Happens When You Deeply Bond With Guys?

We've already talked about sex and virginity ("keeping your fire in the fireplace" of marriage), but what is emotional virginity?

Well, this is where we'll talk about protecting your emotions in relationships with guys. Emotional virginity is probably something you don't think about. But before you dismiss it all together, let's consider the impact it can have.

Ever Been Depressed After a Break-up?

By far, this is one of the most frequent prayer requests I get for teen girls....being broken hearted. It's too common not to address.

If you're a teenage girl, the chances are either you or a friend of yours has experienced feeling depressed after a break-up. Some depression is normal. But, too many girls are getting "stuck" in the hurt and pain.

Statistics have shown a link between sex outside of marriage and depression. But what if you haven't been sexually active?

There are steps you can take to protect your heart.

Are the Gates of Your Heart Wide Open? Has Your "Security Guard" Taken A Break?

Have you been to a gated community lately? Some of you may live in one. They are neighborhoods that have a security guard sitting at a gate deciding who comes in and out of the neighborhood. It gives added protection and security, especially in big cities or high crime areas.

When my husband and I lived in the country of Belize, we lived in a situation like this. Crime tends to be higher in third world countries, so it's more common to have armed security guards at night watching the area. Well, one night we heard a gunshot (our security guard shot straight up in the air to scare off intruders) and came to find out some people had climbed the fence and were coming for our house. That night, I believe the security guard saved us from getting robbed.

What about you? Do you have a "security guard" protecting your heart or is your "security guard" on a break?

The bible says, "Above all else, **guard your heart**, for it is the wellspring of life." Proverbs 4:23

I did a little research on the original Greek meaning of these words. The word guard means "to preserve, guard from dangers, to be blockaded."

And heart means more than just being "mushy, gushy". It is your mind, will, understanding, inner part, knowledge, thinking, reflection, memory, inclination, resolution, determination (of will), conscience, as seat of appetites, as seat of emotions and passions.

I'll repeat it again. "Above all else, *guard your heart*, for it is the wellspring of life."

How Do I Guard My Heart in Relationships?

Most girls like to talk. And talk, and talk. Not all girls are this way, but in general we bond by talking.

Guys are not usually this same way. They bond through adventure and by doing things together. Think of the guys you know, what do they do when they hang out? Watch or play sports. Play video games. Hunting and fishing. Etc.

But, girls love to sit and talk.

My husband knows this about me. I like to talk on the phone with him, but he usually doesn't like it. Why? It's just one of the ways girls and guys are different.

Since girls bond by talking, it's easier for us to share our deepest, most inner thoughts with guys. You talk for hours and it feels like you are bonding so deeply with him. He's such a great listener. But, what happens is, you can open the gates of your heart - too much, too soon. It can leave your heart unprotected and unguarded. If you're married, it could open your heart up to an "emotional affair."

Let's say you tell your boyfriend everything. All your deepest darkest secrets. He's your accountability partner. You trust him completely. Then, 3 months later, you break up. However, he still has a part of your heart. Can he still be trusted with it? Who else will he share those deepest, darkest secrets with? Who do you have to share with now?

Are you starting to understand how sharing too much of yourself too soon can be dangerous?

Is He the one?

You may think that because you are so in love that it's okay to open your heart completely. You think he's the one. But, if you are 14, 15, 16 years old, statistics show that you will most likely not be marrying your high school boyfriend.

That means that it is likely you will break up. And if you do marry him, statistics show that 51% of teen marriages end in divorce before the age of 24. (US Bureau of Statistics)

The bottom line? You will most likely not marry the guy you are dating, so be a very cautious and guard your heart. And if you are married, your heart belongs to your husband, not another guy willing to listen.

Differences Between Guys & Girls

Knowing this ahead of time can save you some pain

There have been entire books written on the differences between guys and girls. Books like "Men are from Mars, Women are from Venus." Doesn't it feel like guys are from a different planet sometimes?

I don't want to stereotype guys and girls because not everyone falls into an exact category. But, let's get a general idea of how guys and girls are different, especially as it relates to relationships.

Guys are Visual

When I was in high school, I remember my dad taking me aside and telling me the differences between guys and girls. One of the things he told me was that guys are visual and attracted to what they see. He said that I could walk into a room with 10 layers of clothes on and a guy could still be turned on by what he sees. That's just the way guys work.

Guys are visual and attracted to what they see. How do we know this? Let's think about this for a moment....who tends to be more addicted to pornography? Guys or Girls? Guys, right? Overall, they tend to be more visual.

Not only that, but their main desire in a relationship is for sex. Simply put...

Guys Are Wired for Sex.

They desire it. It's just the way God made them. "So God created man in his own image, in the image of God he created him; male and female he created them." Genesis 1:27

God gave us sex to enjoy in a committed marriage for the purpose of having children and keeping the earth populated. God says in Genesis 1:28, "Be fruitful and increase in number; fill the earth."

Did you catch that? God gave us sex to ***enjoy***. That's right, ***enjoy***. But, we are to enjoy it within a committed relationship to one person. This is called marriage.

"Marriage should be honored by all, and the marriage bed kept pure, for God will judge the adulterer and all the sexually immoral." Hebrews 13:4

In other words, we are to "keep our fire in the fireplace!" Our fire of sexual passion let loose outside the boundaries of a committed marriage is going to leave damage (broken hearts, depression, STD's, pregnancy, etc.)....just like the damage that would occur if you started a fire in the middle of your bedroom instead of in your fireplace at home.

"May your fountain be blessed, and may you rejoice in the wife of your youth. A loving doe, a graceful deer -- may her breasts satisfy you always, may you ever be captivated by her love." Proverbs 5:18-19

103

Girls long to be loved

We tend to be primarily emotional and long to be deeply loved and accepted. We want the intimacy. That said, we sometimes give sex for love. In other words, we want the emotional bond that comes with sex, not just the physical act. And it does bond deeply! However, it is not God's plan for us.

God created sex to bond us deeply with one man through marriage.

I like the following illustration for the bonding that happens through sex. Try this at home: take out some duct tape and place a 4-5 inch strip on your arm (the side with hair). Make sure it is bonded well with your skin and then pull the duct tape off quickly. Ouch! It probably took some hair with it. Now do that same sequence three more times. What happens? Generally the tape doesn't stick as well the more often it bonds to your skin and then is ripped off.

Can you see where I'm going with this illustration? Sex bonds us the deepest with our first partner; therefore, the bond isn't as deep the more often we casually have sex with many partners.

So, the more times you casually have sex with multiple partners, the less the emotional bond will be. And the less fulfilling sex will be to you as a girl since the emotional bond is primarily what you long for.

Our culture teaches us to give sex for love.

If you are interested in pleasing God with your relationships, it's important to know God's standards on sex.

Not your friends' standards or the standards you see on TV, movies, music videos or the internet. How do we know God's standards? By looking at His Word, the Bible.

Ephesians 5:2-3,5 says "Be imitators of God, therefore, as dearly loved children and live a life of love, just as Christ loved us and gave himself up for us as a fragrant offering and sacrifice to God. *But among you there must not be even a hint of sexual immorality*, or of any kind of impurity, or of greed, because these are improper for God's holy people...For this you can be sure: No immoral, impure or greedy person - such a man is an idolater - has any inheritance in the kingdom of Christ and of God."

I think those verses are pretty self explanatory. We are not to have even a hint of sexual immorality.

Some girls may say...I don't have a relationship with God, so it doesn't matter.

However, because of the differences between guys and girls, girls who give sex for love are making a big mistake. Not only are they choosing to go against God's standards and choosing to sin by having sex before marriage, but they also may not get what they want - the love they were really looking for.

Why? Well, we may think that because sex bonds us to that guy so deeply, he will also have that deep bond and want to stay with us. It's just not the same for the guy. Giving a guy sex is giving him what he wants....he wins.

What happens when you play a video game, or any game for that matter, and win all the levels and know all the secret codes? It gets boring, right? It's no longer as fun to play because it's no longer a challenge.

In a way, that's what happens when we give guys sex. He wins the challenge. The thrill of the chase is over and he may start to grow bored and look for another girl to "conquer." It sounds so shallow, but it tends to be true.

My dad used to say that a girl who lives with her boyfriend is making a mistake, especially if she wants to get married. He said, "Why should her boyfriend ever commit to marrying her if he already has what he wants...sex." He would use this illustration: "Why buy the cow if you can come and get the milk from it every day for free?"

Breaking Up is Hard to Do

Back to the duct tape illustration, which time do you think the tape hurt the worst? Taking it off the first, second or third time? You're right, the first. That's why breaking up with the first guy you've bonded with sexually can hurt so much. Not only that, but you've left part of yourself with him....just like the hair getting stuck to the duct tape. The good news is that you can be forgiven for what you've done (see chapter 22), but unfortunately you can never fully get back that part of yourself once you've given it away.

I John 1:9-10 says, "If we confess our sins, he is faithful and just and will forgive us our sins and purify us from all unrighteousness. If we claim we have not sinned, we make him out to be a liar and his word has no place in our lives."

If you're like me, you may have already messed up in this area of sexuality. I want you to know you're not alone and there is forgiveness for you in Jesus.

If you want a new start, be encouraged that God can give you a fresh start and cleanse you from all your sins.

It may seem impossible to overcome your past or to remain pure from this day forward. But, it's not impossible when you have the power of Jesus at work in your life.

"The reason the Son of God (Jesus) appeared was to destroy the devil's work." *--I John 3:8b*

How Far is Too Far?

The Answer May Surprise You!

Many people claim to be virgins. But, what does that really mean? What is the definition of sex?

Well, to be sure, sex is something that is on everyone's mind...if we'll only admit it! Just read the book of the bible called Song of Songs to realize that people have been thinking about sex for a long time. You may not be thinking about *sexual intercourse* all the time, but your thoughts may be dwelling on a certain guy in your chemistry class and how to get his attention.

Let's face it, there's something inside each of us girls that longs for guys' attention. We like the way they look, the way they smell, the way they talk. There's just something that changes inside of us when they're around. But are there any standards for sex and if so what are they?

What are God's standards for sex?

This is something I wish someone would have clearly explained to me long ago. It would have saved me some heartbreak. And this is something we'll cover later on. For now...

What is the Line - How Far is Too Far?

This is by far the most common question I hear teen girls asking about sex. Many Christian teens have made pledges to abstinence (thinking abstinence means to avoid sexual intercourse only), but want to experiment with other things leading up to intercourse. So, they often want a line in the sand drawn for them of *how far is too far.*

I have to admit that I was one of these girls. I knew I should save sexual intercourse for marriage, but didn't have a strong standard for all the other things leading up to it. So, I compromised with several of my boyfriends allowing things to go further sexually than they should have. Looking back, I now regret those decisions, realizing that one of those encounters even resulted in my boyfriend sexually abusing me. I know God has forgiven me, but I still have had to work through the pain.

This is one of the reasons I feel so strongly about sharing with girls God's standards for sex. I'm not pointing a finger of judgment at anyone; I have been there and gone through it myself. Sexuality has been an area in which God has given me freedom and now I want to lead others to that same freedom I've found.

I'm assuming that you are reading this because you want to please God in this area of your life. So know that I won't condemn you, but I <u>will</u> challenge you to live a higher, godly standard in your sexual life.

I want each of you to know that you are not without help in this area. If sex is already a stronghold in your life, listen to this!

"Though we live in this world, we do not wage war as this world does. Our weapons are not the weapons of the world. On the contrary they have **divine** power to **demolish strongholds**." 2 Corinthians 10:3-4.

God's Standard of Sex - Keep Your Fire in the Fireplace

As I stated when describing the differences between guys and girls, God gave us sex to enjoy in a committed marriage.

Did you catch that? God gave us sex to **_enjoy_**. That's right **_enjoy_**!! But, we are to enjoy it within a committed relationship to one person. This is called marriage.

"Marriage should be honored by all, and the marriage bed kept pure, for God will judge the adulterer and all the sexually immoral." Hebrews 13:4

In other words, we are to keep our fire of sexual passion in the "fireplace" of marriage!

I like this illustration. Imagine your house has a fireplace to provide heat in the cold winter months. Well, let's say that your parents asked you to start a fire when you got home from school. What if you decided to start the fire in the middle of your bedroom instead of in the fireplace? Would your parents come home and think everything was normal. Of course not. And what would be the consequences? You could literally burn your entire house down and be homeless within hours! Talk about being left out in the cold!

Our fire of sexual passion is also designed for the fireplace, the fireplace of marriage.

If our sexual passion is let loose outside the boundaries of a committed marriage, it will leave damage (broken hearts, depression, STD's, pregnancy, etc.)....just like the damage that would occur if you started a fire in the middle of your bedroom instead of in your fireplace at home. What is the moral of this story?

Keep Your Fire in the Fireplace!

"May your fountain be blessed, and may you *rejoice in the wife of your youth.* A loving doe, a graceful deer -- may her breasts satisfy you always, *may you ever be captivated by her love*" Proverbs 5:18-19.

Most of us know that God forbids sexual intercourse outside of marriage. I Corinthians 6:18-20 says, *"Flee sexual immorality.* All other sins a man commits are outside his body, but he who sins sexually sins against his own body. Do you not know that your body is a temple of the Holy Spirit, who is in you, whom you have received from God? You are not your own; you were bought at a price. Therefore honor God with your body."

But knowing where everything else fits into God's standards is where the lines become gray.

"Be imitators of God, therefore, as dearly loved children and live a life of love, just as Christ loved us and gave himself up for us as a fragrant offering and sacrifice to God. But among you **there must not be even a** *hint* **of sexual immorality**, or of any kind of impurity, or of greed, because these are improper for God's holy people...For this you can be sure: *No immoral, impure or greedy person - such a man is an idolater - has any inheritance in the kingdom of Christ and of God.*" Ephesians 5:2-3,5

This is serious stuff - nothing to play around with. If you misunderstand what it means to be sexually immoral, you may risk missing out on the inheritance of the kingdom of God. *Not even a hint.* I know I have not always lived my life according to this standard. How about you?

Webster's Definition of Sex

Let's look at how Webster defines a few sexual terms:

sexual immorality: being unchaste
chaste: innocent of unlawful intercourse
fornication: consensual sexual intercourse between two persons not married to each other
intercourse: physical sexual contact between individuals that involves the genitalia of at least one person.

Did you really read that last definition? I think it's important, so let's read it again. Intercourse is "physical sexual contact between individuals that involves the genitalia of at least one person."

This is where I never fully understood the definition of sex. I always assumed that intercourse meant penetration and penetration only. I was wrong. Even though oral sex and things like mutual masturbation aren't specifically listed in the bible, they still involve the genitalia, which according to the dictionary mean you are having intercourse. Does this definition surprise you? It did me.

So what is included in sexual immorality that God detests?

Here are a few: penetration, oral sex, anal sex, mutual masturbation, petting parties, rainbow circles, hooking up.

112

And if we go back to the verse in Ephesians 5:3 that talks about not having even be a "hint of sexual immorality" we can add other things to our list.

But, on this, I'll let you and God decide.

Stop right now and ask God what actions He considers a "hint of sexual immorality."

_____

_____

_____

_____

_____

Pressured to Have Sex?

I recently had a girl from a Christian school e-mail me this question: *"What if your boyfriend wants to have sex but you don't believe in it and you really love him and can't just leave him. Would it be ok to have sex anyway?"*

I want each of you to know that no matter how much you love your boyfriend or how much he pressures you, God asks you to honor Him by waiting until marriage. You will avoid a lot of heartache and consequences when you do things God's way!!

You have the right to say no to any boy who asks you or pressures you to have sex. Don't be afraid to tell him "No." Even if you have to say it more than once. Any guy who truly loves you will respect your decision and not pressure you. If he continues to pressure you, it may be wise to end the relationship.

Decision Time - Where Will You Draw Your Line Before Marriage?

Will you choose to honor God with this area of romance and dating? Will you decide to reserve intimacy and romance for marriage? Are you ready to surrender this area to God?

If so, you may have developed some habits with guys that will need to change. I can't tell you exactly what this will look like for you.

Some girls decide to save their first kiss until their wedding day. Others decide to avoid being alone with a guy friend they are physically attracted to. This is between you and God.

Hayley DiMarco gives us some suggestions in her book "Technical Virgin, How Far is too Far?"[35] says,

"Below is a list of stuff that you might one day want to do with a guy. They are kind of in a progression, from least sexual to most sexual...Have a look.

- *The Double Take (this is when you oogle your guy and can't stop)*
- *Talking with him*
- *Flirting with him*
- *Touching his arm or leg*
- *Holding hands*
- *Touching each other's faces*
- *Arms around each other*
- *Kissing*
- *Touching below the neck*
- *etc.etc. (I'm not going any farther because I think there's plenty of space above to start drawing your line.)*

So have a ponder. Where will you draw the line when it comes to guys? ...Now talk to someone about your commitment...anyone who will keep you accountable....

Here are some other things and places to avoid if you want to try to keep your line drawn right where it is:

No spending time in your room with him with the door closed.
No napping together.
No lying down together, period.
No hanging out at home alone.
No parking to "enjoy the view" or to "just talk"
No back rubs.
No drinking. (You can lose all memory of lines when you do.)
No dating nonbelievers (They won't have respect for your lines.)

These are just a few situations that can make keeping your line where you've drawn it difficult. So they're things to avoid." [36]

Again, this is between you and God. You have to decide for yourself. But, I strongly encourage you to write down your commitment right now and then share it with at least one person to help hold you accountable and pray for you.

My commitment regarding sex and physical activity with guys before marriage is:

_____

_____

_____

Having a person to keep me accountable in my life has made the difference between having a stronghold and living in freedom in this area of sexuality. I believe the prayers of my accountability partners pulled me through many difficult traps the enemy set up for me.

If you have already made poor sexual decisions and would like to get right with God - do that now. Start by making a decision to change directions and do things differently. Then, ask forgiveness from God as well as forgive yourself (we often forget that!). Go right now to chapters 22 and 23 on forgiveness and repentance for help in this.

I'll close with this, "Put on the full armor of God, so that you can take your stand against the devil's schemes." Ephesians 6:11. I want you to know that I'm praying for each of you, that you will be able to take your stand against the devil's schemes. Please send me your prayer requests, so that I will know how to specifically pray for you!

http://Prayer.TrueBeautyBook.com

 Share Your Thoughts

What do you think? How far is too far sexually? Do you think it is possible to remain pure before marriage and honor God with your sexual choices? What has helped you in your decision to stay sexually pure? Share your opinion and read what others have to say here:

http://Share.TrueBeautyBook.com

Dad, where were you?
God loves me more than any guy can...
by Mandy

I believe that fathers have a very important role in their teenage daughter's life. Unfortunately I never had that father. I have a father and actually he is a pastor of a small church in my town, but he has never been there for me. Ever since I can remember he was NEVER home. I remember countless times when I was younger holding onto my dad's leg as he was walking out, but his job was more important.

By the time I was in 8th grade I was used to my dad not being home, but then a tragic accident happened and he broke his leg so he was home for 15 weeks. I thought to myself, this can be a chance for my dad and I to get closer in our relationship. But, still nothing.

All he did all day was watch TV and expect my mom to be there for him hand and foot. He treated my mom like trash and my siblings and I got to watch all of it. After the 15 weeks had passed by he went to the doctors for a check up on his leg. We found out that he had a blood clot. We also found out that my dad fears dying because after the doctor told him that he could have died if we didn't see him earlier, my dad slowly sank down in depression.

Little did I know that the next three years of my life would feel like a living hell to me and my brother and sisters. He would wake up in the middle of the night and go up to my older sisters room to ask her if she thought he was saved and he would tell her that he wanted to kill himself.

What Christian man and a pastor at that would ask those kinds of questions? Through this time my older sister and I grew closer in our relationship because we were all each other had. Unfortunately, my sister, like a normal girl, needed someone to love her. She needed love from her dad but because she wasn't getting that she searched for it elsewhere.

One day in church there was this kid who knew all the words to say to her. He was her prince charming, but he was a hypocrite. Everything he told her was a lie. He even put on a Christian mask so that my parents would like him. My sister kept slipping though and I watched every minute of it. I was her shoulder to cry on every night when she would cry herself to sleep. I had to go through the torture with her and I was only 14 at the time.

This boy that my sister said she "loved" treated her like trash, but told her that he loved her. Because she got the attention from him she stayed with him and I had to deal with the torture for the next two years. What hurt me the most were the days when she told me that she might me pregnant. I've always wanted to be an aunt but this was way too early. My sister wasn't ready for this.

It was about the second week when we found out that she had miscarried the baby. It was sad but it was for the better. To this day my parents don't know that their oldest daughter was pregnant and I don't know if they will ever find out. My sister went off to college last year and she has progressed so much. I am so proud of her – she has realized that God loves her more than any guy can ever love her. I didn't realize this fact until just a little while ago.

I started going down the same road as my older sister. I craved the attention of boys because I didn't get it from my dad. It all started when my brother and I went to the park to play basketball. I met this boy and he was everything I wanted. He was cute, he was good at basketball, and mostly he

118

liked ME. At that time in my life I had a low self esteem. I never thought I was beautiful and this boy made me feel beautiful.

It started with him just holding my hand and then it went to touching my waist and then he started trying to kiss me. Although I liked this attention deep down I knew it was the wrong attention. My mom told me every day that I was beautiful and I didn't need any guy telling me that.

It wasn't until the beginning of this year that I realized I didn't need guys, but then, unlike my sister, alcohol was an option. It made me feel better it took away my problems at least for a time. But that's the thing...it was only for a time. When I became sober I still had to face the problems.

After crying myself to sleep every night for a month I told myself this was it. I started doing my devos and getting closer to God. This year I have made God my best friend and He's the first to hear about my problems before anyone else.

I have finally realized that God will love me more than any guy can and he will never let me down. Because of His love for me, the least I can do is love Him back.

Ephesians 3:15-19, "I pray that out of his glorious riches he may strengthen you with power through his Spirit in your inner being, so that Christ may dwell in your hearts through faith. And I pray that you, being rooted and established in love, may have power, together with all the saints, to grasp how wide and long and high and deep is the love of Christ, and to know this love that surpasses knowledge—that you may be filled to the measure of all the fullness of God."

Sex and Depression

Is There a Link?

Did you know that research shows a link between sex and depression? It's true. Researchers found that 25% of sexually active teenage girls reported they are depressed all, most or a lot of the time.[37]

What about you? Have you felt depressed lately, but don't know why? You need to realize that research is now finding that guys have the potential to get you really depressed. Especially when taking the self-centered approach to dating.

Check this out...

"One study of 8,200 adolescents, ages 12-17, found that those involved in romantic relationships had significantly higher levels of depression than those not involved in romantic relationships."[38]

Yep...you read that right! Most people think it's more depressing to be alone and single, but research is finding the opposite to be true. Unfortunately, guys will not solve all our problems. In fact, they can create more if we're playing the self-centered dating game and experiencing intimacy without commitment, especially when it comes to sex.

Do you wonder why suicide is the third-leading cause of death for teenagers?[39] Or why "one-third of the adolescent population has thought of killing themselves?"[40] Many times depressing thoughts lead to suicidal thoughts. And what is causing depression in teens? Many things, but sex and romantic relationships is at the top of the list.

Sex is Only a <u>Temporary</u> High

You may think sex is the answer to your problems because it can be fun and exhilarating. But, it's only a temporary high. Short term relief. After that good feeling wears off, you actually are likely to feel *more depressed.*

According to Dr. Meg Meeker who works with many young girls in her practice, "one of the major causes of depression is sex...Teenage sexual activity routinely leads to emotional turmoil and psychological distress."[41]

You Are Not Alone!

One of the reasons I'm writing this book and speaking to teen girls across this country is to let you know *you are <u>not</u> alone*!

I've felt alone many times in my sexual struggles. But, I now realize there are many other girls feeling the same way I do, struggling with the same things I struggle with. One of the reasons I felt so alone in the past is that most people don't talk about sex. It's uncomfortable and a private matter that is not often talked about. Especially in the church.

But, I believe we need to be talking about it. We need to know what God's standards and how He can help us through our struggles. We need to support each other and know that we're not the only ones struggling. To know there are others taking a stand for purity.

So, I'll say it again, "You are not alone."

Breaking Up is Hard to Do

Statistically, if you are a teenager in high school, the odds are your romantic relationships will not last. Very few do at that age. Ultimately there are only two options. Either you will get married or break-up. And since most high school relationships don't last until marriage - you're likely going to break up.

The longer your relationship, the farther you go sexually, the more of your emotions you share....the harder the break-up will be.

I heard someone describe it this way once. It's like you just glued and nailed two boards together. Now, try to pry them apart. There is going to be some damage. The boards are not going to be exactly as they were before. And most likely part of each board will be left on the other one.

That's a picture of what happens when we give too much of ourselves away in a dating relationship and then break-up. It can also feel like an earthquake just destroyed your life.

Sifting through rubble. Incredible feelings of grief, sadness and loss.

Knowing this ahead of time can protect you from a lot of damage. Physically and emotionally. It's easy to say "this won't happen to me. I'm different. I can handle this."

But, what if you knew that when you left your house this morning, you would leave your curling iron on and it would burn your house down. Would you think, "This won't happen to me, I'm different. My house can handle this." No! You would double and triple check to make sure your curling iron was off and some of you might not even use your curling iron anymore.

When we know what the consequences of our actions will be, we are then given the opportunity to decide if we want to change our actions. Are you tired of the cycle of short term self-centered dating relationships? Are you ready to surrender this area of your life over to God?

Confession and Repentance - One Way to See Your Depression Evaporate

Want to see your depression evaporate? One way is to deal with the spiritual side of things. Depression many times can be a result of trying to fill our lives with relationships and things outside of God. So, when we take care of the spiritual side of life, our depression lifts.

Are you ready to take this step? If so, go to chapters 22 and 23 to read more.

Tell us about your break-up.

If you've had a difficult break-up, share your story with us. Wherever you are in the healing process, it's good to know you are not alone.

God is able to heal the brokenhearted and one way He does that is through supporting each other and praying for each other.

http://Share.TrueBeautyBook.com

Overcoming Sexual Abuse

Chapter Eighteen

Healing and Hope After You've Been Deeply Hurt

Even though talking about overcoming sexual abuse is a very heavy topic, we need to address it. There are just too many girls that have been sexually abused to ignore it. Actually, studies and research show that one in three girls are sexually abused before the age of 18.[42] And I'm one of them. The ironic thing is that I didn't even realize it was sexual abuse until 20 years later!

I always thought sexual abuse was intercourse (penetration only) and was usually violent, like rape. But, that's not the case. I believe this is becoming a very widespread problem that not many people are talking about.

So, I'm going to talk about it. I know there is someone out there that needs to hear this. Just like I did.

Have I Been Sexually Abused?

What is considered sexual abuse? We hear of the stories of girls being violently raped by a stranger or sexually molested by their fathers. We know that is sexual abuse. But, what else might be included?

124

Here is a definition of sexual abuse from the book "Healing the Wounded Heart Hope for Adult Victims of Childhood Sexual Abuse." by Dr. Dan B. Allender

"Sexual abuse is any contact or interaction (visual, verbal, or psychological) between a child/adolescent and an adult when the child/adolescent is being used for the sexual stimulation of the perpetrator or any other person. Sexual abuse may be committed by a person under the age of 18 when that person is either significantly older than the victim or when the perpetrator is in a position of power or control over the victimized child/adolescent."[43]

Here's a list from Dr. Allender of the types of sexual abuse and what is considered mild, moderate and severe.

CONTACT:
Very Severe:
Genital intercourse (forcible or nonforcible); oral or anal sex (forcible or nonforcible)

Severe:
Unclothed genital contact, including manual touching or penetration (forcible or nonforcible); unclothed breast contact (forcible or nonforcible); simulated intercourse.

Least Severe:
Sexual kissing (forcible or nonforcible); sexual touching of buttocks, thighs, legs, or clothed breasts or genitals.[44]

Does anything on that list surprise you?

Denial and Rationalization – "It really wasn't abuse", "It wasn't his fault"

If you are anything like me, you really don't want to be labeled as being "sexually abused." It's just not the label most people want. So, when I first started coming to grips that what I experienced was a form of sexual abuse, even though it was "just touching," my first step was to come out of denial and admit what really happened to me.

It hurts to bring up those painful memories, so most of the time we just shove them down and try to forget it ever happened. At least that's what I did.

Then, I was at a women's retreat and the speaker was giving her testimony. She talked about an instance of sexual abuse that was "just touching," but very painful and hurtful to her. She talked about her healing process and how God freed her from the pain.

That day, as she talked, something she said touched on a raw nerve inside of me. It was as if for the first time I was given permission to grieve what happened to me. It was wrong and I had been violated. And it was okay for me to grieve what was taken from me that day. My innocence. My trust.

And I cried and cried. But, they were cleansing tears because for the first time I was able to grieve what had happened to me 20 years ago. I always thought that it was "no big deal" and that it was a normal part of growing up. That it was nothing compared to what some people went through. But, you know what I realized that day? I realized that it was a big deal to me. That it had deeply wounded me....more than I thought. And I needed to heal from it.

Do you know why it hurts so much? Sex deeply bonds us with another person. When we have sexual interactions outside of marriage, we are bound to get hurt. Whether it is a something we choose to do or something that is done to us.

"Flee from sexual immorality. All other sins a girl commits are outside her body, but she who sins sexually sins against her own body. Do you not know that your body is a temple of the Holy Spirit, who is in you, whom you have received from God? You are not your own; you were bought at a price. Therefore honor God with your body." I Corinthians 6:18-20.

I was angry when I realized what this guy had done to me. I didn't want it and yet he still took what he wanted. I realized that I needed to forgive him, although I knew it would be hard.

Getting Help Overcoming Sexual Abuse

If you've experienced any form of sexual abuse, I would recommend talking with someone you trust or considering counseling. I found a good Christian counselor that helped guide me through the healing process. She also recommended this book and workbook, "The Wounded Heart Book and Workbook" by Dr. Dan B. Allender.

More than anything, I want you to know that you're not alone. What is important is that you reach out for help.

The one that can help you the most, God, is the one we tend to go to last. So, talk to Him right now and tell him about your pain and your situation. Everyone is different, so ask God for wisdom on the steps to take that will be the best for you. He wants to heal your broken heart (see chapters 19 & 20).

Share Your Thoughts

What Has Helped You? Wherever you are in the healing process, it's good to know you are not alone. This is a place to help and be helped. So, please give your advice and encouragement on what has helped you in overcoming sexual abuse.

God is able to heal the brokenhearted and one way He does that is through supporting each other and praying for each other.

Share your thoughts and read what others have to say here:

http://Share.TrueBeautyBook.com

Views on Homosexuality,
Is it Right or Wrong?

The song *I Kissed A Girl* by Katy Perry has gotten a lot of attention. As a matter of fact it was at the top of the iTunes downloads for a while.

Why is there such a fascination with two girls kissing? And why is there such a controversy and heated debates over the topic of homosexuality? There are many views on homosexuality, but which do you believe?

To be honest, I really don't like addressing controversial topics like these because it's so easy to be misunderstood. But, I've had this topic come up several times lately and feel it's too important to ignore.

Recently, I was at a teen summer camp and we were traveling in a van to go rock climbing. As we were traveling, I was talking to two of the eighth grade girls sitting behind me. They are both Christians and are involved in the youth group at their church. All of a sudden, they asked me what I thought about homosexuals.

The one girl said her dad was very prejudice about homosexuals and not very nice in the way he responds to them. The other girls said her mom was very judgmental about her friends and judged them by their appearance and not by who they are as a person. And they both disagreed with their parents' judgmental responses.

129

Instead of going right into what I thought, I asked them what they believed

Did they think homosexuality was right or wrong? What were their views on homosexuality?

They both said that although they knew the bible said it was wrong, they didn't see what was wrong with being in love with someone, even if that person was someone of the same sex. They also mentioned that they know homosexuals that are really nice.

Basically, it sounded like they were confused. Their upbringing in the church told them it was wrong, but the culture they live in told them it was okay. So which is it?

Honestly, I don't think these two girls are the only ones confused.

I think there are a lot of people, even Christians, who are unsure how to address the issue of homosexuality in our culture today.

Here are a few lyrics from the song *I Kissed a Girl* that put words to some of the confusion...

"It's not what good girls do. Not how they should behave. My head gets so confused. Hard to obey...I kissed a girl just to try it. I hope my boyfriend don't mind it. It felt so wrong. It felt so right."

Why is the song *I Kissed a Girl* so popular? Quite possibly because it connects with our curiosity and our confusion on this topic of homosexuality.

130

So, what do you think?

What are you views of homosexuality? Is it right or wrong?

Well, as I thought about this very controversial topic, I came up with a few things to consider…

First of all, we've been desensitized

The first time I ever saw two men kissing was at the beach one summer when I was in grade school. I was shocked because I had never seen anything like it before. Not on TV, not in movies, not in public. Nowhere. Until that day.

I still feel uncomfortable seeing two women or two men kiss, but not as much as I used to. Why? Well, I think it's because I've become desensitized to seeing it. You see, over the last several years, the media has started emphasizing homosexuality in our TV shows, songs, movies, music videos, etc.

Think about it…

- Will and Grace TV show
- Boy meets Boy TV show
- The controversial kiss between Madonna and Brittney Spears on MTV Video Awards
- Brokeback Mountain Movie
- California legalizing homosexual marriages
- *I Kissed A Girl* Song

It's everywhere and hard to avoid these days.

It's kind of like walking on gravel. Some people, like me, wear shoes all the time.

131

Therefore, when we walk on gravel, our feet are very sensitive and hurt. However, other people have walked around their entire lives without shoes and have developed thick skin on their feet. Therefore, they can walk on gravel and not even flinch. The gravel doesn't affect them like it does me.

Over time, their feet have become desensitized and calloused.

In the same way, we have become desensitized through the media to homosexuality.

Secondly, different people struggle with different things

You may not struggle with the same sin as I do, but we all have our struggles. I have mine and you have yours.

Did you know that the word "sin" is an old archery term meaning to miss the mark? So, when we sin, we miss God's mark or His standard for our lives.

Some people struggle with drinking too much or using drugs. They may not just drink socially, but they drink to get drunk. I know this was true for me when I was partying in high school. I didn't drink socially...I would drink to get drunk. When I think back on it, I am very thankful that Jesus rescued me from the path my life was going and helped me change directions before it got worse. The bible is pretty clear that we are not to "get drunk on wine, which leads to debauchery. Instead be filled with the Spirit." (Ephesians 5:18)

Some people struggle with lust and have tendencies toward pornography, masturbation, sex before marriage and affairs. Lust can be directed toward the same sex or the opposite sex. Either way, Jesus tells us that lust is a sin. He says in

Matthew 5:8, "But I say, anyone who even looks at a woman with lust has already committed adultery with her in his heart."

Some people struggle with romantic feelings for the same sex and have tendencies toward homosexuality. Some may have been sexually abused by the same sex when they were younger; for example, a guy abused by his brother growing up. This abuse could then open the door for him to be attracted sexually to other men in the future, but doesn't mean that it will. Everyone is different.

Others may have been neglected or abused by the same sex parent growing up, for example, a girl who is physically and verbally abused by her mom. Since she didn't get that nurturing from her mom growing up, it is possible that she could seek it out in other girls, opening the door for her to be attracted sexually to girls, but doesn't mean that it will. Everyone is different and responds differently to hurtful situations in their lives.

We're all different. So we all struggle with different things and cope with hurts in our lives different ways. For some it may be porn, sex outside of marriage, eating disorders, cutting, gambling, cheating, drugs and alcohol, homosexuality and the list could go on and on.

Also, it's not the temptation that's wrong, but acting out on it

We can all understand this concept with a drug addict. They may be in recovery and "not using" but still be tempted to get high on drugs. Just because they still feel the "urge" doesn't make it wrong.

It's their actions that follow that tempting thought that count.

As I mentioned earlier, Jesus said that lust in our minds is a sin, the same as having sex with someone would be. Therefore, is it wrong to look at a beautiful woman or a good looking guy and feel the temptation to lust after her or him? No. It's not the temptation that's wrong, but what you do with it afterward. Do you linger and allow that temptation to turn to lust as you dwell on her or him?

It's what you do with the temptation.

James 1:4-5 says, "But each one is tempted when, by his own evil desire, he is dragged away and enticed. Then, after desire has conceived, it gives birth to sin; and sin, when it is full-grown, gives birth to death."

It happens in steps. It looks like this with one step leading to the next.

1. Temptation
2. Desire
3. Sin
4. Spiritual Death

And it's the same way with feelings toward someone of the same sex. It's not the temptation that's wrong, it's what you do with it. Do you lust after that person and then pursue a relationship with them? Or like the recovering drug addict, do you decide to abstain and allow God's strength to empower you to overcome the temptation?

Next, what is the intended purpose of sex?

Sexual feelings and desires are normal. God created us to have them. Yet, they so often get distorted in our culture today.

Did you know that God created sex?

Yep. He did. God created sex.

How did God create sex? What was the intended purpose?

Genesis 1:27-28 says, *So God created man in his own image, in the image of God he created him; male and female he created them. God blessed them and said to them, "Be fruitful and increase in number; fill the earth and subdue it."*

Genesis 2: 18, 20-24 says, *The LORD God said, 'It is not good for the man to be alone. I will make a helper suitable for him.' ...But for Adam no suitable helper was found. So the LORD God caused the man to fall into a deep sleep; and while he was sleeping, he took one of the man's ribs and closed up the place with flesh. Then the LORD God made a woman from the rib he had taken out of the man, and he brought her to the man. The man said, "This is now bone of my bones and flesh of my flesh; she shall be called 'woman, for she was taken out of man.' For this reason a man will leave his father and mother and be united to his wife, and they will become one flesh.*

I think that God intended sex to be enjoyed...."it's not good for man to be alone." Of course, another purpose of sex is to continue to populate the earth, to "be fruitful and increase in number."

God created sex to be enjoyed in one place....in a committed marriage between a man and a woman.

Some people won't like that statement and will try to dispute the bible.

That's okay. Everyone is at a different place on their own journey and search for truth.

But, I encourage you to really investigate the bible before you decide not to trust it. When I did, I was surprised to find several reasons why I really could trust it as God's Word and live my life according to it. I shared what I found in chapter 23.

But, even beyond the bible, think about it. Does it make sense that sex was intended to be between two guys or two girls?

I was talking to a girl recently who is 25 years old and a lesbian. We'll call her "Beth." She is in a committed relationship with her partner; they have built a house together and are having kids together. Well, kind of.

You see, Beth told me about the emotional roller coaster ride she went on when they decided to have kids. Who would carry the baby? The baby could only be from one of them and then they would have to get a sperm donor to be the father. It was a tough decision. In the end, they decided to have her partner be the carrier. And it was a struggle for Beth. Why? Because deep down, she had a desire to nurture and care for a baby that was her own. A baby that was from her DNA.

Most women naturally have this desire. But, when a lesbian couple decides to get pregnant, there can only be one "true" mother.

Beth said she's pretty confident that her and her partner will stay together. But, if they don't? Well, she has no legal rights to their son because he is not "technically" or "officially" hers.

That's the risk she's taken.

But, as I heard her talk about her story and her struggle, I thought, "Was it really intended to be this way? Did God really create sex to be this way?"

Personally, I don't think so.

Another point to remember: God loves homosexuals. A lot.

In fact he loves drug addicts and liars and thieves and adulterers too. He loves self mutilators and anorexics and porn addicts too. He loves us all. Sin and all.

Romans 5:8 says, *But God demonstrates his own love for us in this: While we were still sinners, Christ died for us.*

But, unfortunately, many Christians haven't displayed this love. Instead they have shown judgment and hate towards homosexuals through the years. And it really saddens me to see how they've been treated. They don't deserve to be called names or ridiculed. They deserve to be loved.

The Church is supposed to be a hospital for sick and hurting people. People with problems and struggles. People like you and me.

Jesus answered them, "It is not the healthy who need a doctor, but the sick. I have not come to call the righteous, but sinners to repentance." Luke 5:31-32

Therefore, we should not be prejudice against homosexuals or homophobic, but show God's love to them. After all, we all have our struggles and need God's grace.

But, we shouldn't stop there. We should also share with them the truth and the hope that is found in Christ.

Finally, what does the Bible have to say about homosexuality?

Is it right or wrong?

Well, to be honest, the bible doesn't say much about this topic. But, there are several references to it.

And the bottom line is that the bible does talk about homosexuality as a sin.

There I said it.

As much as I would like it to be otherwise, I cannot change it.

Homosexuality is a sin just like getting drunk, lying, stealing, adultery, lust, anger, murder, greed…and the list goes on.

It doesn't make it any worse than the other sins. But it still separates us from God. You can read the references for yourself.

Romans 1:24-32 says, *"Therefore God gave them over in the sinful desires of their hearts to sexual impurity for the degrading of their bodies with one another. They exchanged the truth of God for a lie, and worshiped and served created things rather than the Creator—who is forever praised. Because of this, God gave them over to shameful lusts.*

Even their women exchanged natural relations for unnatural ones. In the same way the men also abandoned natural relations with women and were inflamed with lust for one another. *Men committed indecent acts with other men, and received in themselves the due penalty for their perversion.*

Furthermore, since they did not think it worthwhile to retain the knowledge of God, he gave them over to a depraved mind, to do what ought not to be done. They have become filled with every kind of wickedness, evil, greed and depravity. They are full of envy, murder, strife, deceit and malice. They are gossips, slanderers, God-haters, insolent, arrogant and boastful; they invent ways of doing evil; they disobey their parents; they are senseless, faithless, heartless, ruthless. Although they know God's righteous decree that those who do such things deserve death, they not only continue to do these very things but also approve of those who practice them."

I Corinthians 6:9-10 says, *"Do you not know that the wicked will not inherit the kingdom of God? Do not be deceived: Neither the sexually immoral nor idolaters nor adulterers nor male prostitutes nor homosexual offenders nor thieves nor the greedy nor drunkards nor slanderers nor swindlers will inherit the kingdom of God."*

Next Steps...

So if I'm struggling with homosexuality, how do I deal with it?

You deal with homosexuality like any other sin.

You confess and ask God's forgiveness.

And then you repent. That means change directions. Jesus told the woman caught in adultery, "Go and sin no more."

Resources to help

There are resources out there to help you or your friends struggling with homosexuality.

One resource is an online bible study called "The Door of Hope" by settingcaptivesfree.com.

I personally have struggled with lust and pornography, so I took their study on "The Way of Purity." And I highly recommend it. But, they also have a study for those struggling specifically with homosexuality.

The bottom line?

How should we handle songs like *I Kissed a Girl*? Well, I think we should be very careful about the type of media we take in. It really does impact us. And therefore, I think we need to guard our hearts and avoid watching music videos or listening to songs that promote homosexuality, like the song *I Kissed a Girl*.

140

Proverbs 4:23 says, "Above all else, guard your heart, for it is the wellspring of life."

What should our views on homosexuality be? How should we treat homosexuals?

Instead of pointing fingers, let's reach out and throw a lifesaver to those who are struggling with homosexuality....or any sin for that matter. Let's share with them the hope that is in Christ.

Share Your Views on Homosexuality. What Do You Think? This tends to be a controversial topic, even sometimes among Christians. What do you think? What are your views on homosexuality? What are some ways you think we should address this issue?

Share your opinion and read what others have to say here:

http://Share.TrueBeautyBook.com

Part Four

Looking Deeper to Your Heart

Healing the Broken Hearted

Chapter Twenty

"He heals the broken hearted and binds up their wounds." (Psalm 147:3)

"He has sent me to bind up the broken hearted." (Isaiah 61:1)

These verses remind me that there is healing for the broken hearted. I don't know about you, but that comforts me.

To know there is hope.

The verses in Isaiah 61:1-4 have been significant for me on my journey of healing. So, the other day, I decided to study these verses in the original Hebrew language and see what they really mean. What I found was actually quite interesting.

The words "bind up" in both verses come from the Hebrew word, chabash. This word means "to tie, bind, bind on, bind about (like a head band, turban, tiara), to restrain, to bandage."[45]

Did you notice the word bandage? Being a Physical Therapist, I often think in medical terms. So, to think of God bandaging up my wounds is a comforting thought.

The picture I get is of God taking time to personally come and bind up or bandage my emotional wounds. Interesting thought, but that's not all I found.

Stitch by Stitch

The word heal in Psalms 147:3 is the Hebrew word rapha which means, "to heal, to sew together or mend."[46] It's as if God is healing our hurts stitch by stitch.

Have you ever had stitches? Why do we need stitches? What is the purpose of stitches? To hold our wound together so it has time to heal.

That's the picture I get of what this word, rapha – "to heal," does for us emotionally. We can't see emotional healing like we can with a gaping cut on our arm, but God is able to heal us "stitch by stitch."

A Broken Heart Can Cripple You Emotionally

Okay, so let's look at the Hebrew word for broken hearted, shabar, which we find in both of these verses.

"He heals the **broken hearted** and binds up their wounds." (Psalm 147:3)

"He has sent me to bind up the **broken hearted**." (Isaiah 61:1)

Here are a few of the definitions: "to break in pieces, rend violently, crush, rupture, to be broken, be maimed, be crippled, be wrecked, be shattered."[47]

The same word is used in these ways: "Break the door" Gen 19:9; "Break a bone" Exodus 12:46; "Be hurt" Exodus 22:10,14; "Torn" I King 13:26.

Are you getting the picture?

To be broken hearted is to be broken into pieces, crushed, crippled, shattered, and torn. It hurts. Some of you know exactly what I mean.

I see a picture of someone who is in a serious car accident. Because of the accident, their leg bone is shattered. They are crippled and their bone is broken in pieces. But, the doctor comes in to do surgery and puts all the pieces back together. He inserts pins and rods and gives them a cast to wear during the healing process. It is a process of healing and strengthening their leg, but eventually they will walk again.

There is Hope

Do you feel crippled today by your broken heart? Be encouraged and know that Jesus is the "doctor" that can do surgery to bind up and bandage the broken pieces back together and help you heal again. I know what it feels like to be "crippled" emotionally and spiritually for several years. But, I also know what it feels like to be able to "walk again" – experiencing the healing that only comes from Jesus. He restored me. And guess what?

He wants to do the same for you.

When You Feel Broken Hearted

All of us have been hurt at some time in our lives, in need of emotional healing. Whether it's been a bad break-up, parents' divorce, death in the family, abuse, rejection from friends....we've all been there at one time or another.

There have been several times in my life when I was in need of some emotional healing. I want to share with you some of the things that helped me through some pretty difficult times (death in the family, parents' divorce, sexual abuse, etc.).

I wish there were quick and easy emotional healing methods I could share with you that would give you instant healing. I do believe that God has the power to heal us instantly, but most of the time he allows us to heal slowly.

John Eldredge says "If you wanted to learn how to heal the blind and you thought that following Christ around and watching how he did it would make things clear, you'd wind up pretty frustrated. He never does it the same way twice. He spits on one guy; for another, he spits on the ground and makes mud and puts that on his eyes. To a third he simply speaks, a fourth he touches, and for a fifth he kicks out a demon.

There are no formulas with God. The way in which God heals our wound is a deeply personal process. He is a person and he insists on working personally.

For some, it comes in a moment of divine touch. For others, it takes place over time and through the help of another, maybe several others."[48]

Where Do I Start?

Unfortunately, I can't tell you exactly what to do. I wish I could. But, everyone is different and responds differently.

Ultimately, you will need to get in touch with God and ask Him for wisdom on where to start.

James 1:5-8 says, "If anyone lacks wisdom, (she) should ask God, who gives generously to all without finding fault. But when (she) asks, (she) must believe and not doubt, because (she) who doubts is like a wave of the sea, blown and tossed by the wind. That (girl) should not think (she) will receive anything from the Lord; (she) is a double-minded (girl), unstable in all (she) does." *(changed to feminine)*

What Helped Me...

Even though I can't tell you exactly what to do, I can tell you a few things that have helped me the most. Here goes...

I would recommend that you start by reading the next chapters about **forgiveness** and deciding to **change directions**.

Then, by working on your thoughts and the **"stinkin' thinkin'"** that may be going on in your mind (see chapter 6). I know I have had a lot of thoughts and beliefs to change (and still do!).

You may also want to spend time thinking about any habits that may have been passed down to you by your family, **any generational issues**.

If you are struggling with certain habits and addictions, I strongly recommend finding an **accountability partner** or an adult you can trust to meet with and pray with you. It's important to find someone you can trust and I would recommend that your accountability partner be another girl. Things can get fairly messy when you open yourself completely up to a guy.

Finally, you may need to contact a **Christian counselor** and go through some counseling. There have been a couple times I have really benefited from counseling. It's nothing to be ashamed of...we all have times in our lives where we are in need of some extra help and support.

Healing is Possible

Whatever you are going through, it's important to know that Jesus has the power to heal you.

Matthew 4:23
"Jesus went throuhout Galilee, teaching in their synagogues, preaching the good news of the kingdom, **and healing <u>every</u> disease and sickness** among the people."

Luke 6:19
"and the people all tried to touch him, because **power was coming from him and healing them all.**"

Luke 9:11
"He welcomed them and spoke to them about the kingdom of God, **and healed those who needed healing.**"

Matthew 8:7
"Jesus said to him, **'I will go and heal him.'**"

Matthew 8:16
"When evening came, many who were demon-possessed were brought to him, and he drove out the spirits with a word and **healed all the sick.**"

Matthew 12:20
"A bruised reed he will not break, and a smoldering wick he will not snuff out."

Luke 4:18-19
"The Spirit of the Lord is upon me, because he hath anointed me to preach the gospel to the poor; he hath sent me **to heal the brokenhearted**, to preach deliverance to the captives, and recovering of sight to the blind, to set at liberty them that are bruised, to preach the acceptable year of the Lord."

My Broken Heart Restored...

I shared in an earlier chapter that I have experienced an incident of sexual abuse when I was in eighth grade. I didn't recognize it as sexual abuse or even grieve what happened to me until I was an adult.

During that time, with God's empowerment, I began a healing process. It started with forgiveness, which was difficult and not something that came easy for me. One day while I was praying, I began to ask God where He was during that difficult time. (Note: if abuse has occurred, it is recommended to begin visualizing the scene after the abuse has occurred so that you don't re-live the abuse again).

The picture I got was of the guy on the bus taking a knife and stabbing my heart. It was as if my heart was made of glass and shattered into a million pieces the day the sexual abuse occurred. I saw Jesus standing there crying and then lovingly picking up every last piece of my heart.

He showed me the pieces and then said, "You aren't ready for them now, but I'll keep them safe for you." I then saw him put all the pieces of my heart into a safe and lock it with a key.

He said to me, "Shelley, you've looked to your husband and to many other things to heal your heart, but I'm the only one who has the key." Then, he looked at me and said, "_Now_, you're ready."

I then saw Jesus taking out my broken heart and holding all the pieces in his hands. It was miraculously restored and all the broken pieces came back together to form a complete heart. He placed my restored heart back in my chest, but it was still not fully functioning and alive. I then watched him give me "CPR compressions" to get the blood flowing back through my heart again. The blood represented the Holy Spirit which now flows in and through me through my restored heart.

I can't fully explain it with words, but from somewhere deep inside I finally felt "whole" again.

The next week in church we sang the song, "Love the Lord your God with all your heart, with all your strength, with all your mind…" and I sensed God saying to me, "Shelley, now you can love me with _all_ your heart!!" It wasn't an instant fix, but there was something that happened in my heart that day that started a healing process for me.

Forgiveness... God's Maximum Strength "Drano"

Chapter Twenty Two

"Your Tough Clogs Don't Stand a Chance!"

What does Drano and forgiveness have in common? Read on to discover the joy of forgiveness, where your tough clogs don't stand a chance!

Forgiveness is often the first step we take when healing from a hurt. It's also one of the first steps in starting a relationship with God.

What Makes Forgiveness so Powerful?

Let's say you owe a credit card company $15,000 and barely have the money to make the minimum payment each month.

Then, imagine receiving a letter in the mail saying they have forgiven your debt and you no longer have to pay them back. It's cancelled! You'll no longer need to send them payments each month.

What would you be feeling at that moment?

Most likely, it would feel like a huge weight was lifted off your shoulders. That's just a taste of the joy of forgiveness.

The Weight of Unforgiveness

Just like forgiveness can be so powerful, so can unforgiveness.

I heard a story about unforgiveness that I'll never forget. Someone once said that unforgiveness is like carrying a dead person around with you everywhere you go on your back. Eventually what will happen is that *your skin* will begin rotting away from carrying around that carcass.

Sounds pretty gross!

But, that's a picture of what can happen to us when we choose to carry unforgiveness in our hearts toward someone. I know...I've done this before. Emotionally, bitterness and resentment began to take root and eat me away on the inside. I bet some of you can relate.

God's Maximum Strength "Drano"

I John 1:9 is God's maximum strength "Drano." What I mean by that is there are often things that "clog" up our relationship with God. They block our communication with God to where it feels like we're hitting a brick wall with our prayers. Those "clogs" are our sins. The ways that we've missed God's mark or His standard for us.

Back to I John 1:9. It says, "If we confess our sins, he is faithful and just and will forgive us our sins and purify us from all unrighteousness."

Here's the same verse in the Amplified version, "If we [freely] admit that we have sinned and confess our sins, He is faithful and just (true to His own nature and promises) and will forgive our sins [dismiss our lawlessness] and *[continuously] cleanse*

152

us from all unrighteousness [everything not in conformity to His will in purpose, thought, and action]."

I like how the Amplified says it..."continuously cleanse us from all unrighteousness."

I have experienced this in my life. I had allowed some bitterness to take root in my heart and also some unforgiveness towards some people who had hurt me. They were people I trusted which made it even harder.

Finally, I allowed God to come into my bitter and broken heart. The first step for me was forgiveness. Forgiving those that hurt me, asking God's forgiveness and finally forgiving myself.

It felt as if that "clog" between God and I was finally removed! This is when I felt like I wanted to talk to God again through prayer and reading His Word.

The Forgiveness Cross...

1. Forgiving Others
2. Asking God for Forgiveness
3. Forgiving Yourself

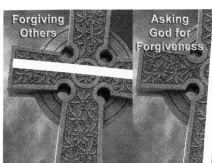 

153

There were three steps I needed to take. If you think about the cross it will help you remember these steps.

First Step: Forgiving Others

First I needed to be willing to forgive those that hurt me. This is the horizontal part of the cross.

For me, forgiveness did not happen immediately and was not easy. It took time, but I knew this was the first step I needed to take.

In forgiving the people who hurt me, I wasn't saying that what happened was okay, but I was releasing the burden of the unforgiveness over to God. He is the ultimate judge and will hold them accountable for what they did to me.

Here are a few verses about forgiving others:

Matthew 6:14-15 "For if you forgive men when they sin against you, your heavenly Father will also forgive you. But if you do not forgive men their sins, your Father will not forgive your sins."

Mark 11:25 "And when you stand praying, if you hold anything against anyone, forgive him, so that your Father in heaven may forgive you your sins."

Next Step: Asking God's Forgiveness

The next step is asking God's forgiveness. This is the vertical portion of the cross.

If you don't know how to pray and ask God's forgiveness, a good place to start is with Psalm 51.

Final Step: Forgiving Yourself

The final step is one we often overlook....it is forgiving yourself. Think about this as the circle at the middle of the cross. I realized that I was carrying around a lot of regret and self condemnation for the mistakes I had made. God reminded me that even though I had forgiven others and had asked His forgiveness, I still hadn't forgiven myself!

What if You Feel Like You Don't Deserve Forgiveness - You've Messed Up Big Time!

Let's say I have a $100 bill. Would you want it? You bet! You could go to the mall and go on a shopping spree.

Well, let's say I take that $100 bill and step on it, rubbing dirt into it. Would you still want it? You bet!

What if I then took that $100 bill and spit on it. Would you still want it? Has it lost any value? Could you still go on that same shopping spree with it? It still has the same high value it started with. It is still worth $100 and can be spent in any store.

Did you know that God sees you the same way?

No matter how much stuff you've been through, how you've messed up or what has been done to you - you still have the same high value God gave you when He created you.

If you've messed up in any area of your life and want forgiveness, it's there for you. The next step I would recommend is to change directions. This is called repentance.

Chapter Twenty Three

Steps of Repentance

If You Are Going the Wrong Direction, Turn Around and Change Directions

In order to start talking about the steps of repentance, I want to share a story with you. One year, my husband and I drove to Florida and on our way stopped to see family in Atlanta. The directions we had said to take 20 East. Well, there was a major interstate in the middle of Atlanta called 20 East. So, we took that road. After driving for 30 minutes on that road, we realized it did not look like the right road.

So, we called our family and sure enough we had taken the wrong 20 East. There is also a 20 East north of Atlanta that we should have taken. We ended up driving an hour out of the way! And in order to get back on the right road, we needed to turn around.

Once we realized we were going the wrong direction, it wouldn't have made sense for us to keep driving in the same direction. It would have just taken us farther and farther from our destination.

Just like we needed to turn around because we got off track driving, if you're going in the wrong direction in your choices, it's time to turn around.

God calls this repentance.

"The Lord is not slow in keeping his promise, as some understand slowness. He is patient with you, not wanting anyone to perish, but everyone to come to repentance." 2 Peter 3:9

When we got lost, our first step was to admit we were lost and ask our family for directions to get back on track.

In the same way, the first step to addressing your issue (depression, poor sexual choices, etc.) is confession - admitting that you've ended up in a place you never intended to go (sexually or otherwise).

Confession goes hand in hand with asking forgiveness. Usually you need to not only forgive those who have wronged you and ask God for forgiveness, but also forgive yourself.

Time for a U-Turn?

Once you've admitted that you are not going in the direction you want, the next step is to turn around. Another word for this is repentance.

Repentance isn't a popular word these days. Our culture encourages us to do whatever we want when we want. TV, music videos and movies very rarely show the consequences of poor choices, they just show the fun and cool side of doing what we want. But, God asks us to *"go and sin no more"* (John 8:11).

Basically, repentance means to stop doing what we're currently doing and start doing something different.

"I tell you that in the same way there will be more rejoicing in heaven over one sinner who repents than over ninety-nine righteous persons who do not need to repent." Luke 15:7

An interesting thing to note, is that the word in that verse, repent, means "to change one's mind for the better" in the original Greek language.[50] I think that's a pretty good explanation of repentance....to change your mind for the better, something different.

Hungry for Chocolate Chip Cookies? Then You Need the Right Ingredients and Recipe.

I believe the same is true in your life. When you are truly ready to repent, you will change. You will need to change "the ingredients and recipe" you've been using in the past.

- Maybe this means you'll begin listening to different music….music that is positive instead of music that has depressing lyrics and just brings you down further.
- Maybe you'll decide to change your PR campaign and the way you dress.
- Maybe you'll change your friends.

One thing is for sure. You'll begin to want to begin filling your mind with God's word and spending more time hanging out with Him and His son, Jesus.

It's hard to change. I know. I've been there….walking down the wrong path and needing to make a U-turn. It didn't happen overnight for me.

At first I didn't want to pray or read the bible. I had no desire. But, I slowly began changing the ingredients in my life. I started to dress and act differently. I began spending more time with God than I did shopping (yes, I am a recovering shopaholic!). I began memorizing God's word to help me overcome my struggles. The list goes on and on…..

But, within one year, I was able to look back on my life and could see how I was a completely different person. My husband could see it. My family could see it. My friend could see it. *When you truly repent and change, people will notice. You will be different.*

Realize that different isn't always bad. Different can be good. When I decided to change, I began to see good things happen.

- A heaviness and a burden I can't even fully express lifted from me.
- Depression lifted from me.
- Bitterness lifted from me.
- And so on.

And in their place entered a freedom, security and love that I can't even express in words.

Are you ready to make a change in your life? If so, let me know. I want to be able to support you and pray for you. We need each other. I look forward to hearing from you. Even though I don't know your name or what you look like, I am praying for you, praying for each person who reads this book. Send me your prayer requests here:

http://Prayer.TrueBeautyBook.com

I believe God has a purpose and plan for your life. How do I know this? He tells me this in Jeremiah 29:11 For I know the plans I have for you declares the Lord, plans to prosper and not harm you. Plans to give you a hope and a future.

Part Five

Find Your True Beauty in God

Does God Speak to Us Through the Bible?

I've been a Christian for many years. And to be honest, I had blind faith in the Bible.

I believed it was God's Word because the Church told me it was. I also had faith in the Bible because it had changed my life. At that time, it was enough for me.

But recently, I went on a journey to find evidence for myself. And I found that there is actually a lot of evidence to back up what I believe in the Bible.

I believe that our enemy, Satan, would like us to think the Bible is full of errors or fairytales. If he can get us to not trust or believe that the Bible is true, we won't have access to the power and freedom that comes from hearing from God through His Word.

So, let's take a few minutes and find out why we can put our full trust in the Bible as God speaking to us.

When we look at a book, how can we know that it's true?

First of all, it really doesn't matter what we believe about it. It matters what is true.

Truth by definition is always narrow. It has one right answer, and many wrong answers. For example, 2+2=4. One right answer, and millions of wrong answers. Another example, one president of the United States. One right answer and billions of wrong answers.

The same concept applies for eternal truth. Eternal truth will also be narrow. We want to make sure we have the right answer. Truth is not what we believed or feel it is. We may believe the sky is green, but it's not. It's blue. We may believe the earth is flat, but it's not. It's round.

So how do we know eternal truth?

I have to admit that I've struggled with accepting the Bible as eternal, absolute truth. As I searched for answers, I found some that makes sense to me.

By the way, many of the concepts I am sharing are taken from chapter three in Mark Cahill's book, "One Heartbeat Away, Your Journey into Eternity."[51] I highly recommend it if you're searching for spiritual truth.

Let me explain to you why the Bible is unique by sharing a few interesting bible facts

#1: The Bible is the best-selling book of all time

How many Bibles, do you think are sold in one year? Any guesses?

150 million! And there are over 4 billion Bibles in print.

Just because the Bible is the best-selling book of all time, doesn't mean it's truth. But, it does mean that it's probably a book that's worth checking into. If that many people are buying it, there's probably something to it.

#2: The Bible claims to be written by God.

All other religious texts were written by men who claimed to be speaking for God. Only the Bible claims to be written by God, speaking to men.

Did you know that over 3000 times the Bible says, "thus saith the Lord."

Knowing that the Bible claims to be written by God, is there any evidence to prove these supernatural words in the Bible? There is. From history, archaeology, science and prophecy we have a lot of evidence to show that the Bible is indeed the word of God. Let's look briefly at it.

#3: Historical evidence

First of all, they are over 24, 000 ancient copies of portions of the New Testament. The closest in all other books is Homer's Iliad, which has 643 ancient copies

Secondly, the Bible itself does not have any contradictions within it. Some people will claim there are contradictions, but when you ask them about it, they have a hard time naming them.

Thirdly, the external evidence for the Bible is incredible. There is a Roman historian named Tactitus and a Jewish historian named Josephus that both support the historical accuracy of the Bible. Also, there were 17 secular historians, who wrote about the death of Jesus by crucifixion. This could not have been made up by men, and shows that external historical records support the Bible.

Finally, no one has been able to identify one historical mistake anywhere in the Bible. If man did write the Bible, we surely would have found mistakes after 2000 years. But there are none.

#4: Archaeological evidence

There have been more than 25,000 archaeological findings relating to people, places, and events in the Bible. And believe it or not, not one of them has contradicted anything in the Bible. That in and of itself is incredible proof of the Bible's trustworthiness.

So if we can believe the historical and archaeological evidence for the Bible, why do you think it's hard for us to believe the spiritual part of the book? Or can we believe the spiritual part of the Bible?

Well, let's investigate and see.

#5: Fulfilled prophecies validate the Bible

Did you know that approximately 25% of the entire contents of the Bible is prophecy. That means about 25%, predicts future events. And to this date, every single one of them has come true to the smallest detail, except the remaining prophecies about the return of Jesus.

Statistically, there is no way any man can predict the future with 100% accuracy. Therefore whom is the only one who can do this?

When someone predicts the future, and then what they say, comes true. And then they predict the future again, and what they say comes true over and over and over again...you can trust whoever it was that predicted the future to 100% accuracy.

The only one that can do this is the God of the Bible, which includes Jesus Christ. We have reason to put our full trust in this book, the Bible, as eternal truth.

What are some of the examples of fulfilled prophecies?

Here are a few...

1. Micah 5:2 says the Messiah will be born in Bethlehem. This is fulfilled in Luke 2:4-7.
2. Zechariah 11: 12-13 says the Messiah will be betrayed for 30 pieces of silver. This is fulfilled in Matthew 26:15.
3. Psalms 22, says the Messiah will be pierced in his hands and feet. This was written about 800 years before crucifixion was ever used as a means of punishment. The New Testament says that Jesus was crucified on across the pierced in his hands and feet.

To finish out...

I want to share something that Mark Cahill shares in his book that will give you a visual image of what we're talking about.

"Jesus Christ fulfilled more than 300 prophecies in his life. Here's something that can help you appreciate the odds of this happening: if only eight of those 300 prophecies came true in any one person, it would be comparable to this:

- Build a fence around the state of Texas,
- fill it 2 feet deep and silver dollars,
- paint one of them red,
- mix them all up,
- then - starting at the Louisiana border – walk blindfolded as far into Texas as you want to go,
- then leaned over, still blindfolded,
- and pick up the red silver dollar.

What do you think the chances are that you would pick up the red one? Would you bet your retirement fund picking up that red Silver Dollar? Would you bet your eternal life on odds like that?

All of us do, because those are only the odds for eight prophecies coming true in one person. But Jesus had more than 300 prophecies about him come true."[52]

How's that for an interesting bible fact?

In closing...

I encourage you to continue your study of the bible for yourself. There are lots of great books out there to get more information from. Eternity is a long time. Make sure you have solid answers for why you believe what you believe!

Connect with God

The Key to Finding Your True Beauty!

We are all on a journey and each of us are at different places in our relationship with God. Some are just exploring who God is and how He can fit into their lives. Some have just begun a relationship with God, while others have been walking with God for a long time.

Wherever you are on your journey, God is close by. He longs to have a relationship with you, but won't force you to spend time with Him.

Feeling Far from God

I have to admit that I went through a time a few years ago where I felt far from God. It felt like there was a wall between God and I. I didn't feel like praying and didn't feel like reading my bible.

Maybe some of you can relate to feeling that way. Maybe you're in that place right now.

For me, I had allowed some bitterness to take root in my heart and also some unforgiveness towards some people who hurt me. They were people I trusted which made it even harder.

Finally, I allowed God to come in to my bitter and broken heart. The first step for me was forgiveness.

Forgiving those that hurt me, asking God's forgiveness and finally forgiving myself.

Then, it felt as if that wall between God and I was finally removed! I truly had a desire to change.

This is when I felt like I wanted to talk to God again through prayer and reading His Word. I actually felt like a sponge -- just soaking up my time with God.

What I've Found Out is That Connecting With God has Helped me Find My True Beauty!

In order to not be influenced by this culture and the media, I realized that I needed to spend more time with God than I was with the culture (including the media).

There are several verses that talk about our need to stay connected to God and be a vessel for Him. Here are a few:

John 15:5 "I am the vine; you are the branches. If a man remains in me and I in him, he will bear much fruit; apart from me you can do nothing."

Galatians 2:20, "I have been crucified with Christ and I no longer live, but Christ lives in me. The life I live in the body, I live by faith in the Son of God, who loved me and gave himself for me."

2 Corinthians 4:7, "But we have this treasure in jars of clay to show that this all-surpassing power is from God and not from us."

Recently, God gave me this picture of what it means to stay connected to Him. It's a picture of a hose connected to the faucet with the water flowing through it and a person watering dry plants.

In this illustration, I am a water hose, a vessel, and the only thing I need to do is stay connected to God, the faucet. When I'm connected to my source, God, His water will flow through me. The water represents His Holy Spirit flowing through me. And Jesus is standing at the end of my hose guiding and directing the flow of the life-giving water to the dry places that need it the most. Just like Jesus guides and directs my life to impact those who are dry spiritually and need Him the most.

Are you connected?

"As the hart pants and longs for the water brooks, so I pant and long for You, O God. *My inner self thirsts for God*, for the living God. When shall I come and behold the face of God?" Psalm 42:1-2 (Amplified)

Think about this question...

When do you feel closest to God?

Whatever it is that helps you feel closest to God, do more of that activity. For me, it's prayer walks. For one of my friends, it is dancing in her room to worship songs. For someone else it might be listening to music, reading the bible or a good book, spending time in nature, being silent, etc.

We are all different, so connect with God the way that works best for you. If you need a "jump start" to getting connected with God, check out the Appendix for some ideas!

Appendix

Ways to Connect With God

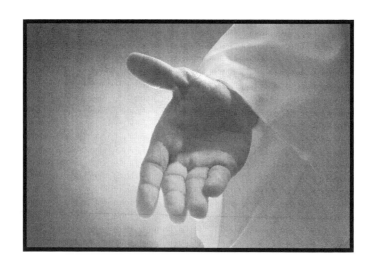

Experiencing God's Presence

(A method by Thom Gardner[53])

1. Go to a quiet place and still your thoughts and emotions (Be still and know that I am God Psa. 46:10)

2. Meditate on a verse of scripture, saying it softly over and over to yourself until you can say it (or a portion of it) with your eyes closed. As you repeat the scripture allow yourself to see it with the eyes of your heart.

    a. What is the picture you see in your mind's eye as you repeat the scripture?

    _____

    _____

    b. What does the scripture reveal about the heart of God?

    _____

    _____

    c. What is the Lord speaking to you personally as you see the truth of this scripture? (Put yourself in the picture of this scripture in your mind.)

    _____

    _____

3. Take time to pray, saying to God what you have seen and heard from Him today.

Scriptures to use with the Experiencing God's Presence method

FEAR - *I am not alone*: Isa. 41:10, Matt. 28:20, Isa. 66:13, Psa. 121:8, Phil. 4:13, Deut. 33:27, Prov. 3:5-6, Gen. 28:15, Jer: 1:8, Isa. 44:8, Deut. 31:6, Josh. 1:9. Psa. 46:7, II Chron. 32:7, Isa. 43:1-2

REJECTION - *I am accepted by my Father*: Deut. 26:18, Rom. 8:16-17a, Isa. 43:1, Jn. 15:15, Rom. 8:31, Isa. 49:15-16, Rom. 8:35-39, II Thess. 2:13, Isa. 45:24-25, Jer. 23:6, Rom. 3:23-24, Rom. 14:17-18, Eph. 1:5-6

WORTHLESSNESS - *The Father approves of me*: Psa. 139:14, Jer. 31:3, Deut. 32:10, Isa. 43:4, Isa. 54:10, Zeph. 3:17, Gen. 1:27, Psa. 100:3, Psa. 119:73, Psa. 139:13-14, Isa. 43:21, I Cor. 15:10, II Cor. 5:17, Eph. 2:10, Col. 3:9-10

SHAME - *I am covered with Christ*: II Cor. 12:9, Isa. 61:10, Isa. 43:25, Psa. 139:7, Rom. 8:1-2, Heb. 2:11, Col. 1:22, Psa. 32:1, Gal. 3:27, Isa. 61:10a, Rom. 13:14

INSECURITY - *I am safe in the arms of my Father*: Psa. 125:2, Isa. 40:11, Psa. 91:4, Psa. 27:5, Isa. 43:2, Heb. 13:6, Psa. 31:14-15, Deut. 33:27a, Psa. 3:1-3, Psa. 32:10, Psa. 34:7, Psa. 121:5-8, Psa. 125:1-2, Jn. 10:27-29

DEFILEMENT - *The Father has cleansed and restored me*: I Pet. 4:10-11, Isa. 63:9, Jer. 30:17a, Lam. 3:22-23, Eze. 16:9, Col. 3:12, Psa. 80:3, Jer. 30:17, Eze. 16:8, Amos 9:14, Nahum 2:2

HOPELESSNESS - *The Truth about hope*: Jer. 29:11, Isa. 43:19, Isa. 58:11, Isa. 50:10, Psa. 18:28, Psa. 30:5, Phil. 4:13, Psa. 130:7, Rom. 8:24-25, I Pet. 1:3-5, I Pet. 1:13, I Jn. 3:3

Praying God's Word

Your Ultimate Weapon

Praying God's word is one way to replace the "weeds" in your life with truth. Beth Moore wrote a book called "Praying God's Word" that has changed my life.

In that book, Beth talks about the power that comes from using prayer together with the Word....

"You and I are just about as effective as the crew with loud mouths, sticks and stones when we try to break down our strongholds with carnal weapons like pure determination, secular psychology, and denial. Many of us have expended unknown energy trying hard to topple these strongholds on our own, but they won't fall, will they? That's because they must be demolished. God has handed us two sticks of dynamite with which to demolish our strongholds: His Word and prayer.

What is more powerful than two sticks of dynamite placed in separate locations?

Two strapped together.

Now, *that's what this book is all about:* taking our two primary sticks of dynamite -- prayer and the Word -- strapping them together, and igniting them with faith in what God says He can do."[54]

How to Pray God's Word to Overcome <u>YOUR</u> Specific Struggle

Your struggle is probably different than mine. Therefore, you can customize this idea of praying God's Word to whatever struggle you are going through.

First identify what struggle is overwhelming you right now. For instance, it could be "fear".

Well, then, you look up verses on the specific topic of fear. I use a concordance in the back of my bible or one online, like www.BlueLetterBible.org.

Once you find some verses that relate to what you're going through, then you re-word the verses into a prayer.

For instance, let's take Isaiah 41:13-14.

I re-worded it to this prayer, "Father, You are my God, who takes hold of my right hand and tells me, 'Don't be afraid, I'll help you. Don't be afraid, Shelley, for I myself will help you.' Thank you, God, that I can depend on You. You don't say 'I might help you, but that You <u>will</u> help me.'"

This concept of praying God's Word is powerful! My prayer is that many of you will begin to apply these two sticks of dynamite to overcome your struggles. Remember...we have been given "divine power to demolish strongholds." (2 Corinthians 10:4)

Memorize Bible Scriptures

Be Prepared for Battle!

When I say the words "memorize bible scriptures", what comes to your mind?

Some of you may be groaning right now because you think about growing up in Sunday School with flannel graphs. Or maybe you have had bad experiences trying to memorize in the past. Maybe you tried to memorize something for a school play and were embarrassed because you messed up in front of a huge audience.

Well, whatever your experience has been, I want to challenge you today to think differently about why it's important to memorize bible scriptures and how it impacts your *true beauty*.

You Are the Bride of Christ....A Warrior Princess!

There is a real battle of good versus evil that you and I face each day. The bible says we are the Bride of Christ and therefore, I like to think of myself as a "Warrior Princess"!

Now, that sounds adventurous and exciting, doesn't it?

So, as a Warrior Princess, think of your sword, your only offensive weapon against our enemy Satan, as the Word of God (Ephesians 6:17 - "...the sword of the Spirit, which is the word of God."). Have you practiced using it lately? Do you know it well?

I know for me, I have felt convicted lately that I am not very *prepared for that battle* I face each day in the spiritual world. As I recently started making an effort to memorize God's word, I noticed that those scriptures would come to my mind just at the time I needed them.

I think of memorizing God's Word kind of like "fencing practice." The only way you get better at it and become more prepared for the real battle is to practice. That's a picture of what we're doing when we memorize God's Word.

Girls, we're getting prepared for the battle!

What Verses Should We Memorize?

The best thing to do is choose verses that relate to what you're going through right now. That's what I do. Then, I'm more motivated to memorize them.

So, if I'm feeling fearful, I memorize verses about fear and trust. If I'm feeling overwhelmed, I memorize verses about God's power to help me. You can use a concordance to look up verses for just about any topic!

Why Do We Need to Memorize Scripture?

Chuck Swindoll wrote, "I know of no other single practice in the Christian life more rewarding, practically speaking, than memorizing Scripture. . . . No other single exercise pays greater spiritual dividends! Your prayer life will be strengthened. Your witnessing will be sharper and much more effective. Your attitudes and outlook will begin to change. Your mind will become alert and observant.

Your confidence and assurance will be enhanced. Your faith will be solidified".[55]

Billy Graham said, "I am convinced one of the greatest things we can do is to memorize scripture".[56]

There are many reasons to memorize bible scriptures, but I want to focus on just one.

Daily Victory Over Satan and our Sin

If for no other reason, think about this...the way Jesus overcame Satan's temptations in the desert was by quoting scriptures (Matthew 4:1-11). If Jesus used scriptures to overcome temptation, maybe we should too.

Psalm 119:9,10 says, "How can a young man keep his way pure? By living according to your word...I have hidden your word in my heart that I might not sin against you."

Ephesians 6:17 talks about "the sword of the Spirit, which is the word of God" as our only offensive weapon against our enemy.

How to Memorize Bible Scriptures Using Music

Adolf Hitler knew the power of music. He said that if you give him the music of the youth of any culture, that he would have that culture in the palm of his hand. His tactic was to change the words of popular anthems to get his political themes into the minds of the young people.

And it worked.

Music can also be used to get God's Word into your mind. Here are a few places you can download songs set to scripture for free!

- www.scripturerelease.com
- www.scripturesongs.net
- www.scripturemusic.com/mp3.htm

Use Pictures to Help You Memorize Bible Scriptures

Have you ever realized that a picture will help you remember something better? They say some people are visual learners, some are auditory learners and some are both.

I've begun to picture the verses I wanted to memorize in my mind. I recently did this with Psalm 91:4 that says, "He will cover you with his feathers, and under his wings you will find refuge; his faithfulness will be your shield and rampart."

I visualized a shield of protection around me. A wall around me where I am safe from harm. I could picture this as an umbrella when it is raining.

So, I then find a picture I am able to use and add the scripture to it to put on my mirror or in a place I'll see it. Here's my example:

He will cover you with his feathers, and under his wings you will find refuge; his faithfulness will be your shield and rampart.
~Psalm 91:4

Other Ideas:

* Write the scripture on your mirror with a dry erase marker.
* Put the scripture on an index card and carry it in your purse or pocket and look at it throughout the day.
* Save the verse in your phone in a note.
* Make the verse your desktop graphic on your computer.

Use whatever works for you!

If we can memorize the lyrics to thousands of songs, we definitely can memorize scripture.

And remember, God is able to help you understand His Word and apply it to your life. Luke 24:45 "Then he opened their minds so they could understand the Scriptures."

If you take the challenge to memorize bible scriptures, I guarantee you won't regret it! It has changed my life.

How has God been working in your life lately? What has He been teaching you through His Word, the Bible? It could be something big or something little. Whatever it is, share it with us and be an encouragement to others.

Share your opinion and read what others have to say here:

http://Share.TrueBeautyBook.com

Scripture Cards

Cut these cards out and put them on your mirror or in a place that you can see them on a regular basis to be reminded of God's promises in His Word for you!

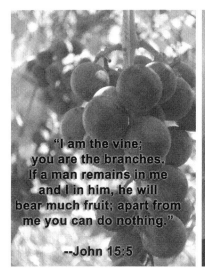

"I am the vine; you are the branches. If a man remains in me and I in him, he will bear much fruit; apart from me you can do nothing."

--John 15:5

"Be Still and Know that I am God."

Psalm 46:10

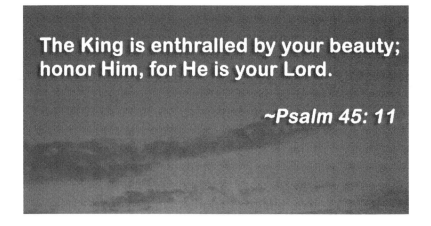

The King is enthralled by your beauty; honor Him, for He is your Lord.

~Psalm 45: 11

Last, but Not Least...
"The Good Test"

Are you a good person...by God's standards? And if so...are you good enough to go to heaven?

Here are a few questions to consider...

Have you ever told a lie?

Have you given money to charity?

Have you gone to church regularly?

Have you ever stolen anything (no matter how small)?

Have you ever used "God," "Jesus," or "Christ," as a curse word? (Example: "Oh my G-d!")

Have you made it a practice to read the Bible regularly?

Have you ever looked at someone and had lustful thoughts?

If You Died Tonight, are You <u>100-percent Sure</u> You Would Go to Heaven? If Yes, How Do You Know That to Be True?

Some of you may already know this, but God has given us a standard to determine whether or not we are good. His standard is called the Ten Commandments. Have you heard of them? You can find them in Exodus 20:1-17.

Let's Go Through a Few of the Ten Commandments Together and See How "Good" We Truly Are...

In the Good Test, did you admit to telling a lie, breaking commandment #9?

I know I did. So, if you're in the same boat as I am, what does that make us? Someone who tells a lie is called a liar, right? So that makes you and I liars.

Let's check out another one.

Did you admit to stealing something in your lifetime, no matter how small it was, breaking commandment #8?

Yep....I confess...I have stolen something in my lifetime as well. If you are joining me on this one, that makes us thieves, right?

So far, not looking so good for us. A liar and a thief. Hmmmm....

Did you admit to having lusted in your heart for someone? Yep...I'm guilty on this one too!

Did you know that Jesus said, "You have heard...'You shall not commit adultery.' But I say to you that whoever looks at a woman to lust for her has already committed adultery with her in his heart." (Matthew 5:28) Therefore, that means we are adulterers at heart!

I don't know about you, but so far I'm not doing so good and we've only covered three out of the ten commandments!

The Bad News...

If we are honest, we have all broken at least one commandment. None of us on our own strength can keep God's standard, the Ten Commandments all the time. James 2:10 says, "For whoever keeps the whole law and yet stumbles at just one point is guilty of breaking all of it."

Bummer!

If we've broken even one of the Ten Commandments, it's as if we've broken them all. That's a pretty tough standard to live up to. That means that Adolph Hitler, Mother Teresa, Osama bin Laden, Billy Graham, you and I...would all be found guilty.

I was amazed to find out that all six billion of us on earth is guilty.

The Security Tag Dilemma

Mark Cahill explains it this way, *"It's as if you had a security tag on your jeans, and you walked out of a store. What would happen?*

The alarm would go off, right?

184

Picture Heaven the same way. At the gates of Heaven, imagine that there are sensors when you try to go in. What is the only thing that will set off the alarm as you try to enter?

Your sin.

Once you leave earth, your sin will set off the alarm. But, if you have been cleansed of all your sin by the blood of Jesus Christ, can you walk through those gates?

Yes!"

It's as if we are all walking around with a security tag on our jeans, representing our sin or the ways we've fallen short of God's standards. None of us meets the standard God has set for us on our own. That means six billion of us are going to be separated from God in a place the Bible calls hell...unless we embrace God's solution to this massive problem.

The Good News...

God does not want you to be separated from Him. You may not have a good image of God for various reasons, but you need to know that He has provided a way for you to be forgiven.

The Bible says that the God of the Universe became a man (Jesus Christ), and suffered and died on the cross for your sins and mine so that we could be set free. Then he rose again from the dead and defeated death! It's as simple as this—we broke the Law, and Jesus paid our fine.

"God demonstrated His own love for us in that while we were still sinners, Christ died for us." (Romans 5:8)

"Christ redeemed us from the curse of the Law, being made a curse for us." (Galatians 3:13)

Being "Good" Does Not Get Us into Heaven

You see, we do not get to heaven by doing good things like donating to charity, going to church or reading our Bible. We cannot earn it, and we do not deserve it, but God is offering it to us as proof of His love for us. We are saved through the sacrifice of Jesus Christ on the cross by grace alone. There is nothing we can do to earn it.

"For it is by grace you have been saved, through faith—and this not from yourselves, it is the gift of God." (Ephesians 2:8)

The Power of Forgiveness

Do you see God's great love for you? Do you see your need for His forgiveness? He is inviting you to come to Him, to be forgiven, and begin an intimate relationship with Him.

Do what He commands and "Repent…that your sins may be wiped out and times of refreshing may come from the Lord." (Acts 3:19)

You must turn away from sin and turn to God. Surrender your life to and put your faith in the One who can save you. Jesus died to set you free, and then he rose from death to be your Lord. Jesus said, "I am the Way, the Truth, and the Life. No one comes to the Father except through me."

If you will confess and forsake your sins (repent) and trust in Jesus Christ as your Savior and Lord, God will forgive you and you'll pass from death to life.

If you are not sure how to pray, read Psalm 51 and make it your prayer.

The Sale of the Year

Here's something else to think about. If your favorite store had a 50-percent-off sale on all clothing today, would you buy anything?

Most of you would.

Now imagine that they had a 99-percent-off sale on all clothing, would you buy anything?

Not only would you probably buy something, but you'd probably get some stuff for your family and friends, right?

So, if you would accept an offer of 99-percent off the price of a piece of clothing, why in the world wouldn't you accept the offer of 100-percent off of all your sin - past, present, and future - washed clean by the blood of Jesus Christ?

It is literally the best deal in the entire universe.

What does it mean to begin a relationship with Jesus Christ?

Let's think of it this way. Let's say you are in an airplane and have to jump 25,000 feet. You wouldn't just "believe" in the parachute; you would put it on! The parachute will do nothing for you unless you decide to put it on, and put your complete trust in it. You know that if you don't have that parachute, you'll die. So, you put it on and trust in it to take you safely to the ground.

187

Starting a relationship with Jesus means to personally trust in Him the same way you'd trust in a parachute if you had to jump 25,000 feet out of an airplane. There are millions of people who "believe" Jesus exists . . . but they have not yet put their trust in Jesus to save them from their sins when they die — there's a BIG difference. And the difference will be obvious when you "jump" through the door of death.

Are you ready to begin a relationship with Jesus today?

Today, I encourage you to turn away from sin, and surrender your life to Jesus Christ. Please don't put it off until later. You probably don't have all the answers to your questions yet, but better to put on the parachute first and then ask questions, than to pass through the door unprepared, grasping for the parachute when it's too late.

If you are making this step for the first time, contact me and let me know. You can e-mail me at shelley@shelleyhitz.com. I want to pray for you and send you some resources to help you grow in your relationship with Jesus

God will transform you from the inside out.

You will think and feel differently as you learn to trust and obey Him. God will give you new strength to live right and love Him above all else.

Start by connecting with God by reading His Word to you in the Bible daily and then begin to obey it.

Still not sure? Have questions?

I'm sure many of you have questions about eternity, heaven and hell. If so, I recommend the book, "One Heartbeat Away, Your Journey into Eternity" by Mark Cahill. You can purchase it at www.markcahill.org.

It is one of the best books I've read on this topic of eternity.

This book provides answers to questions like...

* Can you prove there is a God?
* Doesn't evolution disprove the existence of God?
* Can you prove the Bible true?
* What is out there after I die?

If you would like a copy of "One Heartbeat Away," but can't afford it, please e-mail me at shelley@shelleyhitz.com

I want you to know that I'm praying for each of you that read this book. I pray that you will be able to find the answers to your spiritual questions and connect with God in a real and personal way. I know each of you is in a different place in your spiritual journey, so please feel free to e-mail me your questions.

Bible Study Guide

For Individual or Group Study

Download Free Bible Study Resources:

1) Bible Study Leader's Guide:

   www.FindYourTrueBeauty.com/guide

2) Printable Handouts:

   www.FindYourTrueBeauty.com/handouts

3) PDF version of book (for your iPod, computer or Kindle)

   www.FindYourTrueBeauty.com/ebook

Buy the Audio Book:

MP3 download: www.FindYourTrueBeauty.com/audiobook

MP3 CD: www.FindYourTrueBeauty.com/cd

Buy Additional Copies of this Book:

www.TrueBeautyBook.com

Chapters 1 & 2

"Introduction" & "The Truth About Beauty"

Who or what do you think influences you the most on your ideas of what it means to be beautiful?_____

_____

What role do you think the media plays?_____

_____

Many of us have fallen for this body image lie: *If I could change something about my body, others would finally accept me and I would be able to accept myself.* If you could change one thing about your body, what would you change and why?

_____

_____

_____

What is something you appreciate about the way God made you?_____

_____

Since we are created in God's image, we are created to be beautiful!

How do you think God would define "beautiful"? What makes us beautiful in His eyes? _____

_____

_____

How is that different from man's perspective? (see 1 Samuel 16:7)_____

_____

Reflection/Challenge: What is one thing you could do this week to focus more on your inner beauty instead of just your outer beauty? _____

Journal: (To do on your own time before next week) Read Psalm 139. Write a prayer thanking God for the way He created you.

*Read Chapters 3 & 4 for next week & bring your favorite Barbie or other type of doll from when you were younger!

"The Lord does not look at the things man looks at. Man looks at the outward appearance, but the Lord looks at the heart." 1 Samuel 16:7

Chapters 3 & 4

"Self Esteem" & "Barbie Body Image"

Which statistics on pages 15 & 16 stick out to you the most?_____

_____

Can you relate to Amber's story on pages 17 & 18?_____If so, in what ways?_____

_____

_____

If someone came to you with a similar problem, what encouragement would you offer them?_____

_____

_____

Where are some places you look to find your self esteem?____

_____

_____

_____

"Whatever you do, work at it with all your heart, as working for the Lord, not for men, since you know that you will receive an inheritance from the Lord as a reward. It is the Lord Christ you are serving." Colossians 3:23-24

What can you learn from the above verses?_____

_____

_____

What did you think about the story of Cindy Jackson trying to become "Barbie"?_____

_____

_____

What about you? What influences in your life have shaped the way you view your body (internet/magazines/television shows)?_____

_____

_____

Are there any changes you need to make in your media choices?

_____

_____

Reflection/Challenge: Implement any changes in your media choices (or other choices) that you feel God would have you to make.

*Read Chapters 5 & 6 for next week and feel free to write down in your journal anything that speaks to you.

"The thief comes only to steal and kill and destroy; I have come that they may have life and have it to the full." -- words of Jesus, John 10:10

Chapters 5 & 6

"Body Image Lies" & "Evolution vs. Creationism"

How did Shelley suggest overcoming the lies we believe with God's Truth? (see page 28)

_____

_____

"We take captive every thought to make it obedient to Christ." 2 Corinthians 10:5

Write out the Scripture on page 33 that encourages you the most:

_____

_____

_____

"Healthy self esteem comes from believing in the value God places in you, not in the value man assigns to you."

Did you ever consider that your beliefs about evolution and creationism could affect the way you view yourself and others?_____ If someone believes in evolution, what are some lies they might believe?

_____

_____

_____

Since we DO have a Creator, what are some truths we can believe? (see page 38)

_____

_____

_____

Reflection/Challenge:

1-**Read Chapters 7 & 8 for next week**. When you get to pages 44 & 45, take out the list of lies you wrote out and go through the practical steps to replacing the lies with God's Truth. Please ask someone if you need help finding Scriptures to replace the lies with.

2-Memorize the verse you wrote out earlier from page 33 that encouraged you.

"I like to think of our bodies as the garage for our souls, where we are parked temporarily while we live on this earth. The health, appearance, and abilities of our bodies affect what we do on this earth, but they are not all of who we are. They are significant to us for our time on earth, but will not last for eternity."
-Dr. Deborah Newman

Replacing the lies we believe with God's Truth

Lie	God's Truth
"My physical appearance is the most important thing about me."	"Man looks at the outward appearance but the Lord looks at the heart." 1 Samuel 16:7
"I have messed up too much for God to forgive me."	"If we confess our sins, he is faithful and just and will forgive us our sins and us from all unrighteous." 1 John 1:9
"I don't have any friends."	Jesus is our friend! "I have called you friends, for everything that I learned from my Father I have made known to you." John 15:15
"I have to please or impress others."	"Whatever you do, work at it with all your heart, as working for the Lord, not for men, since you know that you will receive an inheritance from the Lord as a reward. It is the Lord Christ you are serving." Colossians 3:23-24
"I could never do (that)."	"I can do everything through Him who gives me strength." Philippians 4:13

"My life will never amount to anything."	"For I know the plans I have for you, declares the Lord, plans to prosper you and not to harm you, plans to give you hope and a future." Jeremiah 29:11 "All the days ordained for me were written in your book before one of them came to be." Psalm 139:16
"I will not make the right choices for my future."	"Trust in the Lord with all your heart and lean not on your own understanding; in all your ways acknowledge him, and he will make your paths straight. Do not be wise in your own eyes; fear the Lord and shun evil. This will bring health to your body and nourishment to your bones." Proverbs 3:5-8 "If anyone lacks wisdom he should ask God who gives generously to all without finding fault and it will be given to him." James 1:5
"I am all alone."	"God has said, 'Never will I leave you; never will I forsake you." Hebrews 13:5 "The Lord your God is with you, he is mighty to save. He will take great delight in you, he will quiet you with his love, he will rejoice over you with singing." Zephaniah 3:17

Chapters 7 & 8

"Daddy's Little Girl" & "How to Gain Self Esteem"

Do you agree that our fathers have a strong impact on our own self esteem?_____ If so, why do you think that is?_____

_____

_____

How can the way we view our earthly father affect the way we view our Heavenly Father?

_____

_____

You Can Have a Father That Loves You Completely and Unconditionally!

"I pray that you, being rooted and established in love, may have power, together with all the saints, to grasp how wide and long and high and deep is the love of Christ."
Ephesians 3:17-18

What is the 1st step in learning how to gain self esteem? (See page 43, paragraph 2)

_____

What did Shelley call the lies we believe?

_____

One way we can get better at recognizing the lies is to know God's Truth in the Bible so well that we can quickly recognize those thoughts that aren't from Him.

In what ways could you relate to the "Who Am I" poem on pages 48-50?

_____

_____

What are some ways that God has gifted you and that you can "let your light shine"?

_____

_____

Reflection/Challenge:
1-**Read Chapter 9** for next week.
2-**"Let your light shine"** this week.
3-If you haven't gone through the **steps to replacing the lies in your life with God's Truth**, you are encouraged to do so. (See pages 44-45)

"Let your light shine before men, that they may see your good deeds and praise your Father in heaven." Matthew 5:16

Chapter 9

"Fashion Tip: My edition of 'What Not to Wear'"

What would you say influences you the most in regards to the clothes you buy and wear?

_____

_____

Do you agree that compromising in the way we dress can lead to poor choices and actions? _____ If so, how?_____

_____

_____

"Jesus said to his disciples: 'Things that cause people to sin are bound to come, but woe to that person through whom they come. It would be better for (her) to be thrown into the sea with a millstone tied around (her) neck than for (her) to cause one of these little ones to sin. So watch yourselves.'"
Luke 17:1-3

"But I tell you that anyone who looks at a woman lustfully has already committed adultery with her in his heart."
Matthew 5:28

How can the verses above relate to the way we dress?

_____

_____

What is your responsibility in helping the guys around you to have pure thoughts?

_____

_____

Could you relate to Shelley's experience of "drinking from a broken cup"?_____ If so, how?

_____

_____

_____

201

<u>Reflection/Challenge</u>
1-**Read Chapters 10 & 11** for next week.

2-**Create your own challenge** for this week:
"Something I feel challenged by God to do this week in response to this chapter is…"

_____

_____

"Do you not know that your body is a temple of the Holy Spirit, who is in you,
whom you have received from God? You are not your own; you were bought at a price. Therefore honor God with your body." 1 Corinthians 6:19-20

Chapters 10 & 11

"How Are You Advertising Your Body" & "My Journey to Find Modest Swimwear"

When we feel we have to "advertise" our bodies (like cars in the "cheaper car market"), what type of "buyers" will we attract? What might their motives be?

_____

_____

What type of "buyer" will we attract if we are in the "classy car market" and don't feel the need to "advertise" our bodies?

_____

_____

Be a Lamborghini! Even if you've been advertising in the "cheap car market", it's never too late to change!!

Are there any "Modesty Tips" on page 74 that you feel God would like you to work on? What solutions could you try?_____

_____

_____

How about swimwear? What do you think God thinks about your current choice of swimwear?

_____

_____

Are there any ways you feel God would like you to change your swimwear? What are some ways you can do that?_____

_____

Reflection/Challenge:

1-**Read Chapters 12 & 13** for next week. We will begin Part 3: Sex & Dating.

2-This week, every time you get dressed, ask yourself: **"What does God think of this outfit?"** and **"How am I presenting myself to others?"**

"But among you there must not be even a hint of sexual immorality, or of any kind of impurity, or of greed, because these are improper for God's holy people."
Ephesians 5:3

Chapters 12 & 13

"To Date or Not to Date" & "Flirting...Innocent Fun?"

What advice or instruction have you had in the area of sex and dating, and who did it come from?_____

_____

_____

_____

Up to this point, what have your motives been in dating (or wanting to date someone)?

_____

_____

Playing "The Self-Centered Dating Game" teaches us intimacy without commitment and sets us up to continue in this cycle even after we're married...God's standard for us is intimacy within a committed relationship called marriage.

What is "The Little Relationship Principle"? (see page 90)

_____

_____

What are some characteristics of the love God wants us to share with others? (see 1 Corinthians 13:4-8)

_____

_____

_____

In what ways can singleness be a gift?

_____

_____

Some ways I can use my gift of singleness and extra time are:

_____

_____

Instead of worrying about when you'll get a boyfriend or when you'll get married, start enjoying your "Gift of Singleness"!!!

Song of Songs 2:7b says, "Do not

_____ ".

What are some ways we might "arouse or awaken love?"

_____

_____

It's never too late to put your sexuality back to "sleep" until God brings that one person into your life for marriage. It may be difficult, but God has the power to overcome any stronghold in our lives!

<u>Reflection/Challenge</u> from Chapters 12 & 13

1-**Read Chapters 14 & 15** for next week. We'll discuss "Emotional Virginity" and the "Differences between guys and girls".

2-Spend some time this week in prayer asking God what His will is for you in this area of sex and dating. Take some as well as your future husband.
Ask God for wisdom on how to proceed. **Write down your prayer or any thoughts you have. Are you ready to "Kiss Dating Good-bye"?**

3-Consider beginning a journal to your "future husband". You can include your thoughts and prayers for him, Scriptures, etc. This can be really helpful to keep things in perspective as you wait for him and can be a really special gift to give him on your wedding night or shortly after.

Chapters 14 & 15

"Emotional Virginity" & "Differences Between Guys & Girls"

Have you ever felt depressed after a break up?_____ If so, why do you think you felt that way?

_____

_____

How would you define "emotional virginity?"

_____

_____

"Above all else, guard your heart, for it is the wellspring of life." Proverbs 4:23

What does "guard" mean in the original Greek? (see page 98)

_____

_____

What does "heart" mean?

_____

_____

What are some ways we can guard our hearts in relationships?

_____

_____

Statistics show that you will most likely not marry your high school boyfriend, so be very cautious and guard your heart!

Why did God create sex?

_____

"Marriage should be honored by all, and the marriage bed kept pure, for God will judge the adulterer and all the sexually immoral." Hebrews 13:4

What can you do to make sure there is not even a "hint of sexual immorality" in your life? (see Ephesians 5:3)

_____

_____

Reflection/Challenge
1-**Read Chapters 16 & 17** for next week.

2-Create your own challenge from what we've discussed and write it in your journal or on a sheet of paper.

3-Consider beginning a journal to your future husband if you have not done that yet.

Chapters 16 & 17

"How Far is Too Far" & "Sex & Depression"

What is God's standard for sex?

_____

What are some consequences of not keeping the "fire" of our sexual passion inside the "fireplace" of marriage?

_____

_____

"Flee sexual immorality. All other sins a man commits are outside his body, but he who sins sexually sins against his own body. Do you not know that your body is a temple of the Holy Spirit…you are not your own; you were bought at a price. Therefore honor God with your body." 1 Corinthians 6:18-20

Why do you think that sex outside of marriage is linked to depression?

_____

_____

My commitment regarding sex and physical activity with guys before marriage is (see pages 113-114 for ideas of where to draw your line)_____

_____

_____

_____

One person I will share this with and ask to hold me accountable is:_____.

Prayer of commitment to God:

_____

_____

_____

_____

Reflection/Challenge

1-**Read Chapters 18 & 19 for next week**. We'll discuss "Overcoming Sexual Abuse" and "Views on Homosexuality".

2-Share your commitment regarding sex and physical activity with guys before marriage with someone you trust and who will hold you accountable.

3-If you have not done this yet, consider beginning a journal to your future husband.

Chapters 18 & 19

"Overcoming Sexual Abuse" & "Views on Homosexuality"

When sexual abuse occurs, why do you think the victim might try to deny that they were sexually abused or try to rationalize the perpetrator's behavior?_____

_____

_____

What is sometimes the first step in the healing process?_____

_____

Does it make sense that there is a grieving that takes place?_____ Why do you think that is?_____

_____

_____

What are some ways to help someone overcome sexual abuse? (pg. 126) _____

_____

_____

Know that you are NOT alone.
What is important is that you reach out for help.

What are your views on homosexuality?_____

_____

_____

What are the views of those around you?_____

_____

_____

Some things to consider concerning homosexuality:

1.) We've been _____. (pages 130-131)

    a. The gravel concept:_____

    b. _____

2.) Different people struggle with _____
   things. (pages 131-133)
      a. The word "sin" is an archery term meaning,
        "_____"
      b. It's not the temptation that is wrong, but
        _____ on it.

"Each one is tempted when, by his own evil desire, he is dragged away and enticed. Then, after desire has conceived, it gives birth to sin; and sin, when it is full-grown, gives birth to death." James 1:14-15

3.) Look at the _____ purpose of sex. (pages
   134-135)

      a. Why did God create sex?_____
      b. _____
        _____

   What does the Bible say about homosexuality? (pages
   137-138)
      c. Homosexuality is a _____.

"Do you not know that the wicked will not inherit the kingdom of God? Do not be deceived: neither the sexually immoral nor idolaters nor adulterers nor male prostitutes nor homosexual offenders nor thieves nor the greedy nor drunkards nor slanderers nor swindlers will inherit the kingdom of God." 1 Corinthians 6:9-10

   4.) Even beyond the Bible, does it make sense that sex
       was intended to be between 2 guys or 2 girls?
       _____ (pages 135-136)

5.) Remember… _____ loves homosexuals…as well as drug addicts, liars, thieves, adulterers, etc.
    a. How should we treat homosexuals?

_____

    b. How should we handle media that promotes homosexuality?_____

_____

"Above all else, guard your heart, for it is the wellspring of life." Proverbs 4:23

If someone is struggling in this area, how should they deal with it? (page 139)

_____

_____

Refection/Challenge:

1-**Read Chapters 20 & 21** for next week. We'll discuss "Healing the Broken Hearted" and "When You Feel Broken Hearted".

2-Is there anyone in your life who is struggling to overcome sexual abuse or homosexuality? Commit to praying for them this week. If you are struggling with either of these things, talk with God about it AND talk to someone you trust who can help you. Remember, you are NOT alone!

"But God demonstrated His own love for us in this: while we were still sinners Christ died for us." Romans 5:8

Chapters 20 & 21

"Healing the Broken Hearted" &
"When You Feel Broken Hearted"

Have you ever felt brokenhearted?_____

_____

"He heals the brokenhearted and binds up their wounds."
Psalm 147:3

"He has sent me to bind up the brokenhearted." Isaiah 61:1

What encouragement do you receive from these
verses?_____

_____

_____

What is the Hebrew word for "**bind up**" and what does it
mean? _____

What is the Hebrew word for "**heal**" and what does it mean?

_____

What is the Hebrew word for "**brokenhearted**" and what does
it mean?_____

Do any of these definitions stick out to you? In what way?

_____

_____

Be encouraged and know that Jesus wants to heal your broken heart and bind up your wounds.

Where is the best place to start to find healing? (page 146)_____

"If any of you lacks wisdom, (she) should ask God, who gives generously to all without finding fault, and it will be given to (her)." James 1:5

What are some things that might be helpful in the healing process? (pp. 146-147)_____

_____

_____

_____

_____

It's important to know that Jesus has the power to heal you!! "The Lord is close to the brokenhearted and saves those who are crushed in spirit." Psalm 34:18

<u>Reflection/Challenge</u> from Chapters 20-21:

1-**Read Chapters 22 & 23 for next week**. We'll discuss "Forgiveness...God's Maximum Strength Drano", and "Steps of Repentance".

2-Is there anyone in your life who has a broken heart? Commit to praying for them this week and be sensitive to how you can help them. If you have a broken heart, talk with God about it AND talk to someone you trust who can help you. Remember, you are NOT alone!

Feel free to use the space below to write a prayer to God in response to this week's lesson:

Chapters 22 & 23

"Forgiveness…God's Maximum Strength 'Drano'" & "Steps of Repentance"

What are some "clogs" that can block our communication with God?_____

_____

_____

Which Bible verse was referred to as "God's Maximum Strength Drano" verse? (write it out here)_____

_____

_____

_____

_____

What are the three parts of the "**Forgiveness Cross**"?
1.)_____

If we do not forgive others, will God forgive us? (see verse below) _____

> *"For if you forgive men when they sin against you, your heavenly Father will also forgive you. But if you do not forgive men their sins, your Father will not forgive your sins." Matthew 6:14-15*

2.)_____

Psalm 139:23-24 and **Psalm 51** are good passages to read when asking God to search you.

3.)_____

Why is this step sometimes so difficult?_____

_____

_____

What step comes after forgiveness?_____

How would you define "repentance"?_____

_____

_____

> *"The Lord is not slow in keeping his promise, as some understand slowness. He is patient with you, not wanting anyone to perish, but everyone to come to repentance." 2 Peter 3:9*

What is the first step in addressing our sin? (page 156)_____

The word "repent" in Luke 15:7 means...(see page 157)_____

_____

_____

When you truly repent and change, people will notice. You will be different.

Reflection/Challenge

1-**Read Chapters 24 & 25** for next week. We'll discuss "Does God speak to us through the Bible?" and "Connect with God".

2-**"Cookie Challenge!!"**
        You have received a cookie and a recipe card. Whenever you eat the cookie, take out the recipe card and spend some time with God asking if any "ingredients" or "recipes" in your life need to change. You can use the recipe card to write down things or behaviors you'd like to have as "ingredients" in your life (prayer time, reading the Bible every day, only listening to positive music, etc.) and put the card somewhere it can remind you. This activity may lead you to realize you need to go through the steps of forgiveness and repentance in certain areas, so if that is the case, please do so.

Chapters 24 & 25

"Does God Speak To Us Through the Bible?" &
"Connect with God"

Do you believe that the Bible is God's Word?_____ What exactly does that mean?

_____

_____

Do you think we should just have "blind faith" or should we try to find evidence to show that the Bible is true? Why?_____

_____

_____

Some interesting Bible facts:

1. The Bible is the best-selling book of all time
   a. _____Bibles are sold each year (page 161)
   b. There must be a reason so many people buy it!
2. The Bible claims to be written by God
   a. Do any other religious texts claim to be written by God?_____ Who are they written by?_____
      (page 162)
3. Historical Evidence
   a. What historical evidence is there? (pages 162-163)_____

   _____

   _____

4. Archaeological Evidence (page 163)
   a. How many archaeological findings related to the Bible have there been?
   _____

5. Fulfilled Prophecies validate the Bible
   a. How much of the Bible is prophecy?_____ (page 163)
   b. What is one example?_____

   _____

   _____

"I am the vine; you are the branches. If a man remains in me and I in him, he will bear much fruit; apart from me you can do nothing." John 15:5

Why is it so vital that we stay connected to Christ?_____

_____

_____

Are you connected to God?_____

When do you feel closest to God?_____

_____

_____

Reflection/Challenge

1-**Read the Appendix: Ways to Connect with God** for next week.

2-This week, **do more of the activities that help you to feel closer to God**.

Appendix
"Ways to Connect With God"

What method of connecting with God is on page 170?

_____

How would you explain this method to someone?

_____

_____

What method is described as our "ultimate weapon?"

_____

What are the steps for praying God's Word to overcome a specific struggle? (page 173)

1.)_____

2.)_____

3.)_____

What is the last method discussed in the appendix?

_____

You are the Bride of Christ...A Warrior Princess!!

As a Warrior Princess, what is our only offensive weapon against our enemy Satan? (Ephesians 6:17)

_____

What verses should we memorize?_____

How did Jesus overcome Satan's temptations in the desert in Matthew 4:1-11?

_____

_____

Do you think the same could work for you?_____

"How can a young man keep his way pure? By living according to your word...I have hidden your word in my heart that I might not sin against you." Psalm 119:9, 11

What are some ways to help us memorize scripture?_____

_____

_____

What other methods of connecting with God can you think of?

_____

_____

_____

Reflection/Challenge

1-**Read Last, but Not Least... "The Good Test"** on pages 181-187 for next week. This will be our LAST lesson for the study!

2-This week, choose one of the methods of connecting with God and try it...maybe try several and discover which one(s) help you feel closest to God.

Last but Not Least..."The Good Test"

Would you consider yourself a "good person"? Why or why not?

_____

_____

What are the standards called that God gave to Moses & the Israelites in Exodus 20:1-17?

_____

How did Jesus raise the bar even higher? (see Matthew 5:21-22 & 5:27-28)

_____

_____

Have you kept God's commandments perfectly?_____

> *"For all have sinned and fall short of the glory of God."*
> *Romans 3:23*

> *"For whoever keeps the whole law and yet stumbles at just one point is guilty of breaking all of it." James 2:10*

What is the good news in all of this?_____

Why was Jesus the only One who could die in our place? (2 Corinthians 5:21)

_____

_____

Is Jesus the only way to get to heaven?_____ See
John 14:6

*"Jesus answered, 'I am the way and the truth and the life.
No one comes to the Father except through me.'"* **John 14:6**

So how do we accept the gift of salvation? (see page 185)

_____

_____

Think about the "parachute illustration" on page 185. How
can that help us to understand what it means to put our faith in
Jesus Christ?

_____

_____

*"Therefore, if anyone is in Christ, he is a new creation; the
old has gone, the new has come!"* **2 Corinthians 5:17**

<u>**Reflection/Challenge**</u>

1-**Take some time to connect with God each day**, whether
through reading your Bible, prayer, journaling, singing
praises, etc. **Find ways to involve Him in your every day
life**. As you spend time with Him, you will see that your true
beauty comes from who you are in Christ and He can use you
to share this truth with those around you. ☺

2-**Consider sharing your book with someone**. Pray and ask
God if there is anyone in your life who needs to hear from
Him about the topics we've covered in this study.

Shelley's Contact Information:

I would love to hear from you! Send me an e-mail or a letter to the following address:

shelley@shelleyhitz.com
P.O. Box 1757
Findlay, Ohio 45839

Websites:
www.shelleyhitz.com
www.findyourtruebeauty.com
www.truebeautybook.com

Prayer Requests:
Also, send your prayer requests, so that we can specifically pray for you! You can send them to my address above, or submit them through my website online here:

http://Prayer.TrueBeautyBook.com

Fixing our eyes on Jesus,

C.J. and Shelley Hitz

C.J. and Shelley Hitz enjoy sharing God's Truth through their speaking engagements and their writing. On downtime, they enjoy spending time outdoors running, hiking and exploring God's beautiful creation.

To find out more about their ministry or to invite them to your next event, check out their websites at:

www.shelleyhitz.com
www.cjhitz.com

References

[1] Newman, Deborah. *Comfortable in your own skin, making peace with your body image.* Tyndale House Publishers. 2007.

[2] http://www.plasticsurgery.org/media/press_releases/2006-Stats-Overall-Release.cfm

[3] ANRED anorexia nervosa and related eating disorders, http://www.anred.com/stats.html.

[4] Kimberly Shearer Palmer, *Colleges Start to Realize Men Need Body Image Help Too.* USA today, May 10, 2001, 15 A.

[5] "The prevalence of eating disorders." From NEDA. http://www.healthywithin.com/stats.htm

[6] Ibid.

[7] *Coaching the Coaches,* Psychology Today (March/April 1992), 10.

[8] *Searching for the perfect body.* www.people.aol.com/people/000904/magstories/index.html, posted August 25, 2000.

[9] www.kidzworld.comsite/p.3155.htm

[10] Ibid.

[11] Ibid.

[12] *Women spend two-and-a-half years on their hair.* www.dailymail.com.uk/pages/live/articles/news/news.html?in_article_id=402793&in_page_id=1770.

[13] Pendergast, Sara. *Barbie.* Gale Encyclopedia of Popular Culture. 2002.

[14] Ibid.

[15] Norton, Kevin I. *Ken and Barbie at Life Size.* Sex Roles. (Feb. 1996): 287-294.

[16] Jackson, Cindy. www.cindyjackson.com

[17] Pendergast, Sara. *Barbie.* Gale Encyclopedia of Popular Culture. 2002.

[18] Gorchov, Jolie. *Mattel Giving Middle-Aged Barbie a Major Makeover.* LosAngeles Business Journal 20 Mar. 2000. 18 Feb. 2003. www.findarticles.com.

[19] Annika Lampmann (1983) www.Girls4God.de (German Girls Ministry)

[20] Newman, Deborah. *Comfortable in your own skin, making peace with your body image.* Tyndale House Publishers. 2007.

[21] Ibid. p.73

[22] Ibid. p.74

[23] Ibid. p.74-75

[24] Ibid. p.82

[25] Cahill, Mark. *One Heartbeat Away, Your Journey into Eternity.* BDM Publishing, 2005, 15-16.

[26] Ibid. 17-18.

[27] You can purchase Mark's book online at www.markcahill.org/resource.html.

[28] Eldredge, John. *Waking the Dead.* Nelson Books. 2003, p.122

[29] Kylstra, Chester & Betsy. *Biblical Healing and Deliverance:* Chosen Books 2005, p. 141-142.

[30] Gresch, Dannah. *Secret Keeper: The Delicate Power of Modesty.* Moody Publishers. 2005, p. 11

[31] Ibid. p. 48-49.

[32] Harris, Joshua. *I Kissed Dating Goodbye, A New Attitude Toward Romance and Relationships.* Multnomah Publishers, Inc. 2003. p.28.

[33] Ibid.

[34] Ibid. p.39-41

[35] DiMarco, Hayley. *Technical Virgin: How Far Is Too Far?* Baker. 2006.

[36] Ibid. p.134-136

[37] National Longitudinal Survey of Adolescent Health, Wave II, 1996.

[38] Kara Joyner and J. Richard Udry, "You Don't Bring Me anything But Down: Adolescent Romance and Depression," *Journal of Health and Social Behavior* 41 (2000): 369-91.

[39] Armand M. Nocholi Jr., M.D., ed., *The Harvard Guide to Psychiatry*, 3rd ed. (Cambridge, MA: Belknap Press, 1999), 622-23.

[40] A.M. Culp, M. M. Clyman, and R.E. Culp, "Adolescent Depressed Mood, Reports of Suicide Attempts, and Asking for Help,"

[41] Meeker, *Epidemic*, 63 *Adolescence* 30 (1995): 827-37.

[42] Russell, Diana E.H. 1988. The Incidence and Prevalence of Intrafamilial and Extrafamilial Sexual Abuse of Female Children. In Handbook on Sexual Abuse of Children, ed., Lenore E.A. Walker. Springer Publishing Co.

[43] Allender, Dan. 1990. "Healing the Wounded Heart Hope for Adult Victims of Childhood Sexual Abuse." NavPress. p. 48

[44] Ibid. p.51

[45] http://cf.blueletterbible.org/lang/lexicon/lexicon.cfm?Strongs=H02280&Version=kjv

[46] http://cf.blueletterbible.org/lang/lexicon/lexicon.cfm?Strongs=H07495&Version=kjv

[47] http://cf.blueletterbible.org/lang/lexicon/lexicon.cfm?Strongs=H07665&Version=kjv

[48] Eldredge, John. *Wild at Heart.* Thomas Nelson, 2005. p.127-128.

[49] Cross Picture: http://www.sxc.hu/photo/157624

[50] Blue Letter Bible. "Dictionary and Word Search for metanoeō (Strong's 3340)". Blue Letter Bible. 1996-2007. 21 Dec 2007. http://cf.blueletterbible.org/lang/lexicon/Lexicon.cfm?Strongs=G3340&version=kjv

[51] Cahill, Mark. *One Heartbeat Away, Your Journey into Eternity.* BDM Publishing. 2005. Chapter 3.

[52] Ibid. p.79.

[53] Gardner, Thomas. *My Healing Journey.* 2005.

[54] Praying God's Word by Beth Moore. p.6

[55] Growing Strong in the Seasons of Life [Grand Rapids: Zondervan, 1994], p. 61

[56] Personal Thoughts of a Public Man, p.88

4489927R00127

Printed in Great Britain
by Amazon.co.uk, Ltd.,
Marston Gate.